ACTS TO ACTION

THE NEW TESTAMENT'S GUIDE TO EVANGELISM AND MISSION

EDITED BY
SUSAN BROWN SNOOK
ADAM TRAMBLEY

CONTRIBUTORS
JOSEPH ALSAY, CARRIE BOREN HEADINGTON,
FRANK LOGUE, BRENDAN O'SULLIVAN-HALE,
STEVE PANKEY, AND HOLLI POWELL

WITH
JENNIFER BASKERVILLE-BURROWS
FOREWORD
GAY CLARK JENNINGS
AFTERWORD

FORWARD MOVEMENT
CINCINNATI, OHIO

TABLE OF CONTENTS

FOREWORD
JENNIFER BASKERVILLE-BURROWS
BISHOP OF INDIANAPOLIS

For decades, I have been waiting for an Acts 2 Movement, but this engaging and inspiring book has converted me to the Acts 8 Movement. The eighth chapter of the Book of Acts has much to teach us, and the church would do well to dive deeply into it.

In 2008, while serving as rector of Grace Episcopal Church in Syracuse, New York, I met with leaders of the congregation and several graduate students from nearby Syracuse University to wrestle with two simple questions: If you had four hours to give to God in worship and fellowship each week, what would it look and feel like? How might we get outside of our building and bring Jesus into the community?

We were especially inspired by the second chapter of Acts. After the Holy Spirit washes over those gathered for the festival at Pentecost, and after Peter preaches Christ crucified and risen, life among the newly converted is described in Acts 2:43-47:

> Awe came upon everyone, because many wonders and signs were being done by the apostles. All who believed were together and had all things in common; they would sell their possessions and goods and distribute the proceeds to all, as any had need. Day by day, as they spent much time

together in the temple, they broke bread at home and ate their food with glad and generous hearts, praising God and having the goodwill of all the people. And day by day the Lord added to their number those who were being saved.

What could be more compelling than friends gathering in the name of Jesus to break bread, pray, and share all things in common, filled with joy and increasing in numbers day by day? It was everything we wanted our church life to be.

We ended up creating a monthly gathering called The Feast: Potluck Worship. On the fourth Friday of the month, we gathered at a home, park, or other public space for intergenerational worship in the Episcopal tradition. Each month, a different host facilitated the potluck assembly of the worship. Some were in charge of the prayers; others covered music and song. Others saw that a reflection was offered, and still others ensured that we had bread and wine—usually home-baked bread and locally sourced wine from the nearby Finger Lakes region. And, of course, there was a real meal, brought together potluck style. Month by month, if not day by day, the Spirit moved among us. We could barely contain our enthusiasm for inviting others to join us, and our community quickly grew.

Alas, after nearly two years, this ministry faded away. As easy as it had been to create, it proved difficult to sustain. And with a transient community of students and other busy people, the core leadership was not stable enough to hold it together. Those who were part of this froch oxprocsion of ministry in the neighborhood were certainly saddened by its demise, but our enthusiasm for being formed by and following in the Way of Jesus was not diminished. But I wonder now if we had meditated on more of the Book of Acts and taken inspiration from Chapter 8, we might have been more prepared for disruption and change in even this nascent effort to proclaim the gospel and embody Christian community.

When the Acts 8 Movement first came together in 2012, I was still an Acts 2 person, but I was curious about these folks who had found inspiration and motivation in the whole of the Acts account, and particularly in Chapter 8. I knew Scott Gunn, Susan Brown Snook, Brendan O'Sullivan-Hale, and other members of this network from around the Episcopal Church, and I became curious about what they were up to. I was taken by the questions they were asking and their belief that the Episcopal Church might move through a challenging moment in its history and become the vital, transformative, loving communities of Jesus followers that God has been calling us to be from the very beginning.

In the pages that follow, the authors delve into the rich accounts of the early church and explore its struggles to remain viable, withstand persecutions, and navigate theological differences. And in doing so, they show us that there is more than just comfort to be found in knowing that we've been here before. By making connections between the earliest days of the church and our own time and place, the authors guide us in exercises that invite us to reflect and explore, both individually and communally, how God is acting in our midst.

Acts 8 is for both a mature church and new followers of Jesus. It invites us to the deep work of formation and reflection that has always been part of the Christian life but is even more critical now, in this age when our challenges mirror those of the early church and when we too are being called to be disciples of Jesus who take nothing for granted. Read thoughtfully and engaged thoroughly, this book can take us on a journey that will give us not the church we've always wanted but the church God most needs us to be.

INTRODUCTION
SUSAN BROWN SNOOK

It is a difficult time for the church. Social forces have impacted believers in such a way that it's not clear how the community of faith can continue. The institutions that have held the church together are breaking apart, and people have scattered, unsure of their next step, uncertain whether the gospel will survive into the next generation.

The Christian church in the twenty-first century? No. This is the scenario facing the followers of the Way in Jerusalem, 40 CE. These early followers of Jesus encounter seemingly insurmountable obstacles: persecution, uncertainty, doubt, and fear. Yet empowered by the Holy Spirit, the handful of early followers share the good news of Jesus Christ far and wide. These few faithful followers start a worldwide movement, one of hope and joy and the promise of abundant life.

The description of those early days in the church might sound familiar to us. The Episcopal Church and indeed most mainline denominations in North America face some grim realities: Attendance is declining, sometimes precipitously, our membership is aging, and many of our financial resources are drying up. The population of North America is growing rapidly while many of our churches are shrinking, demographically looking less and less like the surrounding neighborhoods. We flounder, not sure how to reach the people God loves so dearly. Yet there is great hope and possibility. We believe that the gospel, the good news of Christ, is a vital message for all to hear. God's love for us is so intense that it led Jesus Christ, the Son of God, to come into this world and live and die for us; it is a love so unconquerable that God raised Jesus from the dead; a love so eternal that God sent the Holy Spirit to us so that God's love would grow and spread throughout the world. This love is worth sharing with those around us. But how do we accomplish this mission when our church structures seem to be faltering, when we are unsure of a way forward, when we don't always understand the good news of God in Christ ourselves?

We can look for answers through the spiritual disciplines all Christians are called to: prayer, scripture reading, worship, giving, serving others, and discernment of our mission in community. We can also look to the 2,000-year story of the church to see how God has led Christians on this path before. And when we do, we find that the followers of the Way have confronted similar challenges from the very beginning. We find their story—and our story—in the New Testament Book of Acts.

As Acts opens, the resurrected Jesus speaks his last words to his friends before he ascends into heaven. These words in Acts 1:8 are in a sense the mission statement for the entire Book of Acts, a foreshadowing of how the story of the church will unfold. Jesus says, "But you will receive power when the Holy Spirit has come upon you; and you will be my witnesses in Jerusalem, in all

Judea and Samaria, and to the ends of the earth." This mission statement draws a picture of concentric circles: Jerusalem at the center, the familiar country of Judea surrounding it, the unfamiliar enemy territory of Samaria beyond that, and the unknown wilds of the ends of the earth extending to the entire known world and beyond. This is an overwhelming mission, but Jesus doesn't think small. The Holy Spirit comes with power, and the gospel is going to spread.

The apostles create an organization in Jerusalem, one with assigned roles and delegation of responsibilities to deacons and others. This method of organization has been highly successful, baptizing thousands of people who are inspired by the story of Jesus. By the power of the Holy Spirit, the apostles preach in the temple and gather large crowds of believers. The whole structure is growing, reaching new people and seeming to portend a great revival in religious life in Jerusalem. Then, just before Acts Chapter 8, the crisis comes. Stephen speaks out of turn, insisting that the older temple organization is not necessary. Stephen is killed for his words, and a persecution begins. The fledgling institution is destroyed and scattered, and no one knows what to do next.

No one, that is, except the Holy Spirit. Where human plans fail, God is doing something new. It turns out the very persecution that scatters the believers and destroys their institutions becomes the seed of new life in unexpected places and ways. The twelve apostles have assumed that the main life of the church will always continue in Jerusalem, headquartered in the temple. But the Holy Spirit flings the church out into new and frightening places: Samaria and the road to Gaza and a place called Azotus. The Ethiopian eunuch becomes a Christian and heads back home, carrying the gospel with him to a place the apostles would surely think of as "the ends of the earth." Baptism happens in a puddle of water alongside a road, instead of in a carefully planned liturgical ceremony.

Sharing the gospel of Christ rarely happens in a smooth, graceful progression. The apostles have successes and setbacks. They work wondrous miracles and make rookie mistakes. They struggle with each other over different interpretations of their mission, and they struggle to follow the lead of the Spirit in fits and starts. They fail to take literally the mandate from Jesus to go to "the ends of the earth," and they stay in Jerusalem where they are comfortable—until they just can't stay there anymore.

These early followers face the same challenges that we do today. Like the first apostles, we know how to be the church in the familiar surroundings of our own temples, our own "Jerusalems." What we're not sure of is how to be the church outside our walls, even in the familiar "Judeas" of our neighborhoods and among people similiar to us. We're even less sure of how to interact with our unfamiliar neighbors, the "Samaritans" who might be of different races or social classes or political outlooks or life experiences or religious (or non-religious) backgrounds. Yet, we are called to reach them. We must reach them if our churches are to thrive, but we don't know how. We are indeed in the midst of being scattered, flung headlong into a new world.

Acts Chapter 8, the story of how the first disciples respond to challenges similar to ours, provides rich and fertile ground for us to discover how to meet today's crises. This book studies the events of Acts 8 and explores how we might apply its lessons to the life and mission of our churches today. Many of the contributors to this book are members of the Acts 8 Movement, a group of Episcopalians dedicated to mission, evangelism, and discerning the call of the Holy Spirit in our church today. The Acts 8 Movement was established before the Episcopal Church's 2012 General Convention by Scott Gunn, Tom Ferguson, and me to be an advocate for change in the church.[1] Since 2012, Acts 8 has continued to grow and evolve as a loosely organized yet passionate group of advocates for evangelism and prayer in the Episcopal Church.

Out of our zeal for sharing the good news of Christ, we offer this book, which explores the lessons of Acts Chapter 8 and offers them as a model for church mission today. We hope the book is used by individuals and in group study; discussion questions and practical exercises can help individuals and congregations discover how to answer their calling from the Holy Spirit. The book is divided into four sections, based on the four fascinating stories we find in Acts Chapter 8. At the beginning of each section, we explore in greater depth the scriptural story. Then building upon these stories, we look at essential elements of church mission in the twenty-first century.

---

[1] Read the original blog posts announcing this new movement: http://www.acts8movement.org/founding-blog-posts/.

The first section looks at the change that comes to the church as a result of the persecution of Stephen and how this change brings new focus to the proclamation of the gospel. Then we explore Philip's trip to Samaria and how his proclamation opposes evil and brings joy. The third section concentrates on the curious story of Simon the Magus, with lessons about the changes that come to us in repentance and the power of prayer. In the last section, we hear the beautiful story of Philip and the Ethiopian eunuch, which reminds us of how to read scripture and how to work to understand our own communities.

Ultimately, these stories in Acts Chapter 8 share a common thread of relational evangelism and beg the question: How do we share the good news of Christ that we have experienced with the people we meet in the course of our ordinary lives? Every congregation must confront this vital question as we consider how to accomplish the mission that Jesus still gives us: to be his witnesses in our churches and in our neighborhoods, among people we know and trust, among people who are different and strange to us, and ultimately, to the ends of the earth.

SECTION ONE
ACTS 8:1-4

And Saul approved of their killing him. That day a severe persecution began against the church in Jerusalem, and all except the apostles were scattered throughout the countryside of Judea and Samaria. Devout men buried Stephen and made loud lamentation over him. But Saul was ravaging the church by entering house after house; dragging off both men and women, he committed them to prison. Now those who were scattered went from place to place, proclaiming the word.

THE STORY
BRENDAN O'SULLIVAN-HALE
HOLLI POWELL

The eighth chapter in the Acts of the Apostles could be summed up in a phrase from Lin-Manuel Miranda's musical *Hamilton*: "This is not a moment; it's the movement." At the beginning of the chapter, those who have placed their hope in a light shining in the darkness are themselves on the verge of being snuffed out. By the end of the chapter, the faith has escaped the confines of Jerusalem, carried out into cities and the wilderness alike by Christians with hearts enflamed by the Spirit.

The Book of Acts was written by Luke as the second volume of a series. The first volume, the familiar and beloved Gospel of Luke, tells the story of Jesus' life, from birth to resurrection. The second volume, the Acts of the Apostles, picks up where the Gospel of Luke leaves off, with the resurrected Jesus about to ascend into heaven. From this point, the followers of Jesus have to learn how to be the church and carry on Christ's mission without his physical presence. They start out in Jerusalem and organize a successful missional community there. But at the end of Chapter 7, Stephen is stoned to death, and at the beginning of Chapter 8, a persecution against the church in Jerusalem scatters the followers of Jesus into the countryside.

The first few verses of Acts Chapter 8 are a geographic pivot as definitive as the change in direction toward Jerusalem in Luke's account of the Transfiguration. After teaching his disciples that "those who want to save their life will lose it, and those who lose their life for my sake will save it" (Luke 9:24), Jesus ascends a nearby mountain to show Peter, James, and John his divine authority in the event we know as the Transfiguration. From that moment on, each step Jesus and his disciples take is in the direction of Jerusalem and toward the cross.

The death of Stephen recalls the Transfiguration, only the geographic direction is reversed. Testifying before the high priest, Stephen's face "was like the face of an angel" (Acts 6:15). In the moment before the assembled crowd seizes him, "he sees the heavens opened" (Acts 7:56). Finally, turning his spirit over to Christ as stones rain down on him, Stephen cries out for the forgiveness of his murderers, showing himself transformed through the imitation of his Lord.

From the moment of Stephen's transfiguration, the steps of Christ's followers move away from Jerusalem and out into the wider world, as most of the Christians flee Saul's persecution. Human nature would lead many of us to flee Saul's rampage against Christians and start over elsewhere, quietly, not making a fuss or causing a commotion in our new town. But these Christians go from place to place, boldly telling the story of their faith to everyone who will listen. Saul's attempt at shutting down the practicing believers backfires spectacularly, as his tactics inadvertently encourage the spread of Christianity beyond Jerusalem.

But not everyone leaves Jerusalem. The apostles stay behind for reasons that are unknown to us. Immediately before the Ascension, Jesus instructs them "not to leave Jerusalem, but to wait there for the promise of the Father" (Acts 1:4). Still, they are clearly aware that the gospel promise is to go well beyond Jerusalem. Pentecost brings the gift of the Holy Spirit to the apostles, but some of the crowd sneers and assumes they are drunk. Peter urges the crowds to repent and be baptized, assuring them that the promise of forgiveness and the gift of the Holy Spirit is "for you, for your children, and for all who are far away" (Acts 2:39).

For whatever reason, a new set of believers who have never personally met Jesus are the ones to carry the message out of Jerusalem and into the world. Perhaps, having been companions of Jesus, the apostles lack the imagination and vision for how to build the church without his physical presence and guidance. When Thomas doubts the resurrection without physical proof, Jesus answers: "Blessed are those who have not seen and yet come to believe" (John 20:29). These early Christians spread their faith with no proof of the resurrection other than their own transformed lives. Why do those who have never known Jesus in person carry the church's mission forward? Maybe they are the only ones who can imagine the way forward being passed from person to person, sparked by the Holy Spirit. Their way focuses not on direct experience of the physical incarnation of Christ but on his message: the gospel and its power to transform us all.

CHAPTER 1: SIGNS OF THE TIMES
STEVE PANKEY

As the eighth chapter of Acts begins, things are looking pretty grim for the fledgling Jesus Movement. One of the seven deacons in the church has been martyred, a full-on persecution has begun, and the church in Jerusalem is hemorrhaging members. The first three verses of Acts Chapter 8 should come with a warning label. *CAUTION: What follows will likely induce hand-wringing anxiety.* Despite what seem to be dire circumstances, the script flips almost immediately. "Now those who were scattered went from place to place, proclaiming the word." In Luke's original Greek, we see that they are preaching the good news, evangelizing as they go. Given the signs of the times, this response seems counterintuitive. What motivates the earliest followers of the Way to overcome their fear, doubt, and anxiety, so that even while they are fleeing persecution and death, they continue to evangelize? What can the Episcopal Church learn from this moment in the early life of the church?

If you are reading this book, you don't need a chapter full of statistics to prove that things aren't going well in the life of the church. I should know: I wrote that chapter, and the editors sent it back. What we need instead is a chance to look afresh at the signs of the times through the lens of the church of Acts Chapter 8, to see things in a new and hopeful way. How do we take what looks like a moment of desperation and turn it into an Acts 8 Movement? From the church in diaspora in Acts 8, we see that this type of radical movement requires honesty, imagination, and a whole lot of faith.

Being honest about where we are as a church is a two-sided coin. Yes, we have an obligation to take an honest look at our current situation, like that desperate moment in Acts 8:1, but we also must be willing to name the good in this moment as well. Having promised you that this won't be a chapter full of statistics, I'll simply point out that with which most of us are already familiar. The Episcopal Church, along with Christian denominations across the theological and liturgical spectrum, has experienced a prolonged period of steady decline. In my decade of ordained ministry, I have felt this most acutely in the experience of those who consider themselves regular church attenders. In 2007, I would have told you that our Sunday regulars showed up at least every other Sunday. Now, it seems every third Sunday suffices for many regulars. Priests look out upon congregations that are less full of less active folk.

Unlike the early church, this decline is not because of intense persecution. Rather, my sense is that we are in the midst of profound cultural shifts, with constant demands on time and attention. As a church, we have been apathetic about our faith, failing to show by word and example the difference that Jesus makes in our lives. The church has not helped people see, in the midst of all the demands upon their time, why a relationship with Jesus matters.

This apathy is a dangerous symptom in a desperate moment. As we learn in the first verses of Acts 8, the Christians who flee Jerusalem have every reason to slip quietly and politely into their newfound homes. An apathetic faith would suit them well in a time of persecution, but it would be disingenuous. Instead of quietly going about their lives, those who leave Jerusalem take their enthusiastic, outspoken belief in the power of Jesus with them. They did not hear him teach or watch him die or touch his wounds, but the power of the resurrection is alive and well within them.

Like the apostles of Acts Chapter 8, we Episcopalians have not heard Jesus teach, watched him die, or touched his wounds. It would be easy to go about our lives with only a cursory nod to Jesus from time to time. We could slip into apathy; we could decide that our faith is worth only an hour a week to us, perhaps less. Or we could follow the witness of the apostles in Acts Chapter 8, naming the power of God's transforming love in our lives and sharing our enthusiasm about Jesus' love with others.

In my experience as an Episcopal priest, the most fervent evangelists are often new to the Episcopal Church. A couple in my congregation in Alabama had been devoted Lutherans in every city in which they had ever lived. They had run food pantries, been involved in prison ministry, and even planted churches, but when they arrived in town, there was no Lutheran congregation. After some searching, they found their way to us. We were, in their words, "the best Lutheran congregation around." Immediately, they began to invite their neighbors to worship with us. One couple one week. Another couple the next. This went on for months. Some tried us for a week and never came back. Others found something they had been looking for. Eventually, almost 10 percent of people in church on Sunday mornings had been invited by this one couple. Their excitement about their new community of faith was honest and authentic. They had found something they wanted to share. And they were willing to do so!

Those who flee the persecution of Saul take their excitement about Jesus with them from place to place as they search for a new home. They are authentic in their story. Given that they are fleeing imprisonment, these new Christians can't claim that following Jesus is an easy path. Yet their willingness to share the good news no matter the cost becomes a powerful witness that this newfound life of faith is worth the risk. As they take the stories of their transformed lives in Jesus to new communities, Jews in Judea and Gentiles in Samaria, these evangelists shape their story in ways to connect with different audiences. Almost immediately, sharing the gospel message requires the gift of imagination.

We can assume that most of the followers of Jesus who leave Jerusalem take with them only their stories. As they enter new towns, they have an opportunity to share them. In a world that isn't as mobile as ours, moving is rare. Newcomers are treated as honored guests. They have the chance to bring news from their travels to their new community. In Jewish cities, the newcomers may be invited to address the synagogue. In Gentile territory, small groups of Jews might be eager to hear what is happening in Jerusalem. In each new context, the story of Jesus' death and resurrection is likely shared a bit differently, but its core message of love, salvation, mercy, and grace remains constant. This is a valuable and exciting lesson for us today: The gospel of Jesus doesn't change, but the methods by which we share that good news must be adapted to the audience.

Too often, leaders attend a conference on the topic of church growth and return with a canned program that can be opened, microwaved, and spoon-fed to their congregation. This method is, of course, ridiculous. Every congregation is different, and a program that suggests it can be lifted from one context and placed upon another without any imagination or adaptation isn't worth spending a penny on. Instead, only after an honest evaluation of our congregation's strengths and weaknesses, opportunities and threats, can leaders begin to do the imaginative and prayerful work of developing a program of discipleship and evangelism that will work for their community. Sometimes, this strategic work happens in a large, overarching manner, but more often, it occurs piece by piece, as needs arise.

When I arrived at my congregation in Alabama in mid-2007, they had a longstanding commitment to the Catechesis of the Good Shepherd as a Sunday school curriculum for children. Teachers were trained on an ongoing basis. Dues were paid every year. Thousands of dollars had been spent to set up the classrooms with felt boards, sandboxes, communion sets, and other supplies. On any given Sunday, six teachers were prepped and ready to teach. And on most Sundays, attendance in the program was about four children. As I familiarized myself with the congregation, I learned from vestry minutes that the church had struggled for more than fifty years with low attendance in Sunday School. Everyone—vestry members, clergy, and parents alike—wanted a Sunday school program to rival the Methodists. The church had poured resources (finances, time, and people) into having everything teachers might need to share the story of God's saving grace with children. And for five decades, the needle never moved. Sunday school attendance remained low, and teacher morale slipped even lower.

It was time for an honest and imaginative conversation about children's Christian formation. We started with our Sunday school teachers. They felt exhausted and disappointed. It was disheartening for them to put so much work into something and then see so little participation. While the teachers loved the program and the children with whom they worked, they were ready for a change. They needed a change. So, we made a change. Actually, we tried a lot of changes.

Eventually, after several conversations over several years with our teachers, our elementary-age children, and their parents, we heard two things loud and clear. First, offering the formation classes at 9 a.m. on Sunday was not working. Asking parents of small children to get out the door an hour early was a fool's errand. Second, parents were desperate to hear a sermon without wrangling wiggly kids. We made the difficult decision to end the 9 a.m. Sunday school hour. It was sad; it felt risky. We were nervous, but we had listened to the people, we had tried several options, and we were willing to be imaginative.

What resulted was a new initiative we call Follow the Word. Similar to a children's chapel program, the children gather around the Gospel book as it is being read, and then they carry the book out into the parish hall. While a preacher offers the sermon to the rest of the congregation, the celebrant and a volunteer lead an age-appropriate conversation on the gospel lesson along with a simple art project. At the time of the offertory, the children come to the altar and present to the congregation what they have learned. Volunteers sign up to help once every eight weeks or so. Parents are able to listen to the sermon, and children receive age-appropriate theological education. As a side benefit, even first-time visitors see their children engaged and learning about Jesus.

I know this isn't a one-size-fits-all solution—I wouldn't want it to be! This solution worked for us. Our community was located in one of the fastest-growing counties in America. We had two clergy on staff, which meant one priest stays with the adults while another priest joined the children, showing that their education was just as important as the adults who stayed to hear the sermon. We also had folks who were comfortable with kids moving around and the occasional possibility of glue oozing onto the fair linen. Still, even with these advantageous circumstances, it took us fifty years to come up with a new solution. Fifty years! The turning point in finding a new way was the willingness to have honest conversations about what was and wasn't working. We committed to spending time in imaginative and prayerful discernment about how we might bring the good news to our children in new and accessible ways and to have faith that God would be faithful to us. As a result, our congregation grew. What had been the source of fifty years of anxiety could have gotten the better of us, but in faith, we stepped out, seeking ways to share the message of God's saving grace with children of all ages.

In my current parish in Bowling Green, Kentucky, the context is quite different. The city is ten times larger. We are a distinctly downtown parish. Our neighbors are the city library and two looming towers of low-income apartments. In the late 1980s, the church entered into a period of discernment. Would they commit to being a downtown parish or was the siren song of the suburbs calling them? As the story has been told to me, the decision was clear: Christ Episcopal Church belonged in downtown Bowling Green. Some thirty years and two $1-million-plus capital campaigns later, I inherited a congregation with plenty of space and desire to be a downtown church but still discerning what this means in its day-to-day life.

One way that we have tried to respond to the call to serve the community is through our Wednesday Community Lunch. In our downtown context, we see poverty and chronic homelessness every day. The Wednesday Community Lunch began five years ago with a simple intention: feed anyone who was hungry and wanted to share a meal. We would open the doors to anyone— not just the college professors and attorneys that are plentiful in our downtown community but also to the homeless at the library and the residents of the low-income apartments across the street. The community lunch was launched with the goal of taking the good news of

Jesus beyond Sunday morning by sharing our resources with our diverse community. Today, the Wednesday Community lunch has evolved and grown, with twenty volunteers feeding about 100 people each week. This initiative has forced us to ask difficult questions about building use, safety, and propriety. It has created more than a few moments of fear and discomfort, but it has also opened our eyes to the possibilities God has in mind for the world we see changing around us.

The story of the church during the persecution of Saul could easily be about the power of sadness and fear. If it weren't for the faith of those who fled, Christianity might have ended with the martyrdom of Stephen—another apocalyptic sect, a blip on the radar. Thanks be to God, that is not the story of Acts. Instead, Acts Chapter 8 tells a story of faith despite seemingly insurmountable odds, a story of the power of hope in a world hell-bent on destruction. Those who flee Jerusalem do so out of fear for their lives, but they never give up on their faith in Jesus Christ. They take with them the amazing stories of Jesus, of healing and love and grace. They tell these stories—they evangelize—every place they go. They offer the word of salvation to all. Individually, these stories are small acts, but collectively, they change the world. The church expands to Judea, Samaria, and eventually to the ends of the earth.

Two thousand years later, we are facing a similar moment of fear and anxiety. While our lives may not be at stake, the church to which many of us have devoted our lives struggles to survive amidst threats both from the outside world and perils of its own design. We have a choice. We can live in fear and apathy and watch our church slowly fade into obsolescence. Or with God's help, we can make this a moment of opportunity. With faith in God's steadfast faithfulness and love, this moment calls us to go out into the world, exploring new and imaginative ways to share how the good news of Jesus Christ has transformed our lives. The foundational story of the church is a story of faith in the midst of uncertainty, a willingness to be open and honest about God's power in the lives of the faithful, and the power of the Holy Spirit to inspire the imaginations of the faithful in the proclamation of the gospel. Inspired by the faithfulness of Christ's earliest followers, we too can share the love of God in our neighborhoods and experience what it means to bring great joy into our cities.

FOR REFLECTION AND DISCUSSION

- What struck you in this chapter about the examples of the congregation reading and responding to the signs of the times?

- What areas of your faith life and your church's life are depressed or depressing? What might it look like to reimagine those areas?

- How would your congregation change if everyone acted like the church's greatest challenges could be its greatest opportunities?

- How would you define "bringing great joy" into your community?

FOR ACTION

- Talk with at least two people who have been in the congregation for a long time. Ask them what in the church's life and ministry has made the biggest difference for them. Share what you learn with others.

- Talk with at least two people who are new to your congregation. Ask what brought them to your congregation and what kept them coming back. Share what you learn with others.

CHAPTER 2: WORSHIP
JOSEPH ALSAY

Acts Chapter 8 is a pivotal moment in the story of the young church. The church has been gathered in Jerusalem, awaiting the coming of the Holy Spirit, and then making disciples through the power of the Spirit. These disciples gather in the temple, worshiping, hearing the word of God, performing miraculous healings, and baptizing thousands of people. The gathered church is wildly successful in Jerusalem, until the persecution that follows the death of Stephen sends the disciples out to new places. It turns out that being sent into unfamiliar places allows the disciples to gather new communities of faith in new ways. Over and over in our lives, we are gathered into the presence of God and sent out again to do God's work. An important part of this gathering and sending is rooted in our weekly worship.

On Sunday, the first day of the week, Christians have assembled for two millennia to observe rituals, to sing and say words, and to participate in holy actions. What is amazing and absolutely astonishing is that in this post-modern age of television and the demise of most small public assemblies, this regular meeting survives. In some places, it even thrives, being held near and dear to the participants. Why is that? What does this meeting mean? How do the traditional words and symbols make any sense or offer help amid the constant flood of demands in our modern time? Is this "go-to-church-meeting" Sunday gathering— the liturgy, the mass, the worship service—simply the leftovers of a collection of quaint customs? Or does worship itself offer us a realistic pattern for interpreting our world, for sharing our actual experiences, and for enabling action and hope?

In many churches, the weekly occurrence of worship is treasured as the very heart of Christianity. It is the primary way in which the people of God gather in the presence of God to remember and reenact God's love for us.

The meaning of liturgy resides first of all in the liturgy itself. If the gathering has a meaning for us, if it is an authentic thing about God and our world—indeed, if it brings us face to face with the holy otherness of God— then that becomes known while we are participating in the gathering. The liturgical vision engages us while the order of actions flows over us, and we perform the patterns of this public work.

We—the church—are continually gathered and then sent out as part of our worship. In this, we follow Jesus, whose earthly ministry involves cycles of gathering and sending: gathering the twelve, sending them out, gathering them again, sending them out again. Gathering them and breathing upon them. Gathering them after the resurrection and commissioning them to be sent into all the world. Gathering them with the other disciples, in Jerusalem, and sending the Holy Spirit upon them. Sending them out to tell the good news to others.

In each part of our worship, we are gathering and sending. In the service of the word, we open with acclamation and call to worship. God gathers the people by the power of the Holy Spirit. True, the gospel is preached and the call to worship goes forth through human lips and hearts, but it is God who moves hearts and motivates feet to join in worship. In the midst of this gathering, our hearts and minds are shaped by the gospel. At the end of the service of the word, we offer the sign of peace. The peace is a sending: We are being sent to reconcile. As Saint Paul writes, we are "agents of reconciliation." But we are sent into the service of the sacrament first.

In the Holy Eucharist, we are nourished by Jesus' body and blood. The Great Thanksgiving gathers us again, this time around the holy table. Christ invites us to his meal. Our meal ends with the post-communion prayer and a dismissal, sending us out into the world to love and serve the Lord. Within the liturgy, we gather and send. We reflect this eucharistic pattern each time we sit down for a meal. We gather with family or friends, we bless our food, and we eat together. Then we are nourished and sent along on our various callings.

In all this gathering and sending, a great mystery operates, the mystery of the gospel and the Holy Spirit that transforms those who gather so that they can be powerfully sent. We who gather are human, part of the mundane life. We are also a mystical body that is spiritual and physical. We are human beings, and we are filled with the Holy Spirit. The church is founded on people, the apostles and prophets and Jesus himself. It is a structure, a historical institution. And yet it is also a holy temple, a dwelling place for God. So, everything we do when we worship is fully human, and yet as the Body of Christ, it is filled with the Holy Spirit. Sadly, in our modern mode of knowing, we are pulled toward binary thinking. We feel we are supposed to choose whether the church is spiritual or human. It is both.

It is amazing that through our worship, the church, in a unique way, can be a vehicle to show that the Spirit is still living, breathing, and powerful. It can show the world that its message is inspired and offers a unique expression of the Story of our Creator God and the redemptive plan. It unlocks human hearts. The sacrament is the same. It is bread and wine. It is the Body and Blood of Christ. It is the common made holy.

We, the people of God, when we worship in common, are made holy. The form of this world, its patterns of thinking, its goals, its desires, its ruthlessness, and its selfishness pass away. So, we are redeemed and sanctified. We are filled with the Holy Spirit, and yet we are being filled. We are sinners; we are saints.

As we take on the call to gather in worship, we do human things. We sing, we talk, we bow, we eat, we bathe, we drink. Real water, real tables, real wood, real bread and wine are used in the worship of the triune God. Yet, as we consume the Body and Blood of Christ, as we hear the very word of God speaking, as we receive God's very presence, as we become a temple for the Holy Spirit, God moves. God moves in us. God is with us as humans. God is transforming us, not erasing us. As God moves further into our hearts, God moves us further out into the world, sending us to take what we have experienced to those outside our walls.

This is a great mystery, and at the same time it is part of everyday, human life to worship God. I once heard it said, "Humans without traditions will create them." I believe this is true. On Sunday, the great task and opportunity, indeed the great privilege, laid before us is to be so daring as to open the treasure troves of our forebears and bask in the timeless, stunning beauty of being gathered and sent. Let us never forget that worship is a verb. It is practiced and lived out. It is not merely theoretical: This devotion and praise of the faithful, gathered by the Spirit, and sent into the world is the true heart of worship. Granted, the act of worshiping God in Christ is not complicated. Yet our intention and attention to these simple actions are crucial.

When I came to St. Augustine's of Canterbury in Oklahoma City, the congregation had dwindled to a handful of the faithful. The search committee wondered, "We know you are a high-church guy. St. Augustine's has never been high church. How are you going to make that work here?" I answered that I love the signs and symbols that are part of a more traditional liturgical practice, whether incense or candles or colorful vestments. But my hopes for liturgy are deeper than a particular style. I follow three major principles in creating our worship, which I call the three r's. Worship must be real, relevant, and reverent.

REAL

In too many churches, we have reduced the great signs and symbols of the church to tiny, inconsequential things. A loaf of bread has become a Chiclet-size cracker. A chalice of wine has become a jigger of grape juice. A river of water has become "a little drop'll do ya." I believe liturgy should incorporate the real. Here's a litmus test: Give the eucharistic bread to a child. The child will tell you the truth. Does this break like bread, look like bread, taste like bread? The signs and symbols of the liturgy should give us a foretaste of heaven. Water should be used in abundance. Wine should be full-bodied. If you use incense, the smoke should billow out. I want to see it, smell it, taste it.

Don't be afraid to use art and color. Remember that in the Middle Ages, the church was the original patron of the arts. For far too long within many Protestant churches, the notion of using the visual arts as a means of grace or vehicle to experience the wonder of God has been shunned. But our God is a God not just of order but of absolute beauty. Just take a look at nature, and you will see that truth. Beauty should be an integral element of worship. God has given a talent to artisans. Look back to the Book of Exodus, to the details given for the creation of the tabernacle, the traveling sanctuary of God. Using the arts for worship is a way that artisans can praise and glorify God, who is the giver of all good gifts.

Another key ingredient in dynamic worship is the role of music. An African proverb says, "The spirit will not come down without a song." Music is a universal language that can transport us to another realm. Indeed, it can often speak far more eloquently than words, expressing the deep longings of our hearts. Music must be chosen carefully and with an awareness of the context and culture in which it will be addressed and performed. Music that speaks to our minds, hearts, and souls passionately and beautifully helps craft a liturgy that is real, that touches people where they are. Trying to find music that reaches across the vast cultural expanse of St. Augustine's can be a challenge at times. But so far, the congregation has been willing to try something new and open to how the winds of the Spirit are blowing.

RELEVANT

When I first came to St. Augustine's, we formed a liturgy and worship committee. After every liturgy, we ask the question: Why are we doing this? We tweak the liturgy often because worship needs to be relevant to people's lives. It needs to be catechesis, that is, teaching, because worship is our primary opportunity to impart our faith to others. Episcopal priest Sandye Wilson has said, "Faith is not so much taught as it is caught." If the primary time for the community of faith to gather and have the story transmitted to them is worship hour on Sunday morning, how will the story of the faith be transmitted to them? Everything we do in the liturgy needs to convey the absolute essential truths of our faith, from the words of the sermon to the symbols of the sacraments.

I believe that our corporate worship has the ability to empower people for evangelism in the world. But I hold the deep conviction that this can only happen if the worship is Spirit-filled and culturally relevant. The people of God come together to be prepared and equipped for ministry. It is an opportunity to be fed so that we are propelled back into the world to make a difference. Worship should prepare people for the challenges they face and the ministries they perform.

REVERENT

Worship brings us into the presence of God. It confronts us with the "holy otherness of God." We don't need to engage in a particular set of church practices to be reverent. But in many places, the church has lost its sense of mystery, the awe and wonder we should feel when in the presence of the God who made heaven and earth. In the Orthodox church, when the priest begins to chant the opening tones of the liturgy, you don't have to understand the words to know you are entering a new space: Time ceases to exist, and everyone present is swept up into worship that has gone on in heaven since time immemorial. Our reverence reminds us that we are standing in the presence of God, joining with angels and archangels in the heavenly chorus.

Worship has the ability not only to transport us to a different spiritual place but also to transcend culture. If you attend a church full of people who are very different from you, who engage in worship practices that are not familiar to you, nevertheless at some point you will find a point of community as brothers and sisters. In the Episcopal Church, our *Book of Common Prayer* unites us across many cultures. In a broader sense, we are all children of God. The old spiritual goes, "In Christ there is no East or West, in him no South or North, but one great fellowship of love throughout the whole wide earth." Our worship should be reverent because the community that is formed there, transcending cultural divides in the presence of God, is the very symbol of God's kingdom among us.

Worship should be real, relevant, and reverent. It should incorporate music and art. It should equip the people of God to do the work of God in the world. I truly believe inspiring worship is key because worship gathers and empowers the community. Most likely it is during worship that guests and newcomers will experience who we are as a community of the faithful. And certainly, it is from there that Christians will be sent out into the world to do Christ's work. My father once said that you can know what a congregation believes through their worship. How true his words are!

FOR REFLECTION AND DISCUSSION

- What in this chapter made you think about worship in a new way?

- Can you think of a time you understood yourself being gathered by the Spirit to come to worship? Can you think of a time that you left worship knowing that you were being sent out to do something?

- In what ways do you find your congregation's worship to be real, relevant, and reverent? In what ways could your congregation's worship become more real, relevant, and reverent?

- What would be different if the entire congregation felt it was being commissioned by God at the end of every Sunday worship service?

FOR ACTION

- Jot down notes during worship of ways God might be calling you to be sent out to take action.

- Ask a few others (either those in your church or, better yet, friends from outside of church) to gather with you for worship and then to meet afterward and talk about where God might be sending you together to love and serve.

SECTION TWO
ACTS 8:5-8

Philip went down to the city of Samaria and proclaimed the Messiah to them. The crowds with one accord listened eagerly to what was said by Philip, hearing and seeing the signs that he did, for unclean spirits, crying with loud shrieks, came out of many who were possessed; and many others who were paralyzed or lame were cured. So there was great joy in that city.

THE STORY
BRENDAN O'SULLIVAN-HALE
HOLLI POWELL

Luke, the author of Acts, narrows his focus from the broad to the specific in this passage by following one of the many scattered disciples. Philip has not been a major character in the narrative up to this point. His only previous mention is as one of the seven, along with Stephen, chosen to feed the poor in Acts 6. But Philip goes to Samaria, even though there's not much reason for him to expect a warm welcome. After all, a Samaritan village refused Jesus entry on his journey to Jerusalem (Luke 9:52-56). And tension between the Samaritans and the Jews is a repeated theme in the gospels. But the unexpected occurs: Philip is received in Samaria with joy.

Philip's calling as a deacon informs how he spreads the gospel. A deacon's ministry, as described in *The Book of Common Prayer*, is "to represent Christ and his Church, particularly as a servant of those in need." Long before these words were written, Philip lives them out, proclaiming the Messiah by relieving suffering, bringing the kingdom of God near. It's the kind of proclamation foretold in Luke 4, when Jesus reads the scroll of the prophet Isaiah, who says, "He has sent me to proclaim release to the captives and recovery of sight to the blind, to let the oppressed go free, to proclaim the year of the Lord's favor." It's a proclamation of the good news of Jesus, not just in words, but perhaps more critically, through Philip's actions among the people of Samaria.

In his epistle, James writes, "Faith by itself, if it has no works, is dead" (2:17). He is criticizing a later group of Christians who make an intellectual assent to Christ's authority while simultaneously showing favoritism to the wealthy and dismissing the poor. Philip shows us what a true faith looks like: tangibly changing lives, healing the sick, curing those plagued by demons, and causing the paralyzed to walk. Philip is hands-on. He is in the thick of life in all its messiness, and he is meeting the people of Samaria exactly where they are.

We don't often see evangelism as a mechanism for bringing joy and delight, yet this isn't a new idea. In a 1954 reflection on the topic that could as easily have been written today, the Rev. Theodore P. Ferris writes:

> The arrival of a Christian missionary in a non-Christian community is like the gathering of storm clouds... Quite the contrary is true, however, wherever real Christianity is concerned. It always brings joy, for it is comparable to releasing a man from prison...One of the best tests that can be suggested for a Christian church in a community is this: Are the people rejoicing because it is there? If they are not, then that church might well re-examine its life and character.[2]

Philip's ministry with the Samaritans passes this test, for as verse 8 of this chapter tells us, there was great joy as a result of his time among them—great joy, brought by one unknown Christian, led by the Holy Spirit and his love of Jesus, to a place filled with people struggling and in pain.

---

[2] Ferris, Theodore P. *The Interpreter's Bible* Volume 9, p. 109, 1954 Abingdon-Cokesbury Press.

CHAPTER 3: PROCLAMATION
FRANK LOGUE

Preach the gospel at all times; use words if necessary. This much-quoted phrase attributed to Saint Francis of Assisi repackages the saying "actions speak louder than words" by harnessing it to proclaim the good news of what God has done through Jesus. Rather than stating that we need to practice what we preach, this saying declares we will find words superfluous if our deeds are in keeping with the gospel.

Let's dig a little deeper into this saying as we consider how our proclamation can make a difference. Francis was certainly changed through experiences, perhaps more than through preaching. The son of a wealthy textile merchant, Francis was born in 1182, into a new Italian middle class coming into its own. His father's wealth and Francis's own natural charisma made the young man a leader of the youth of his town.

Francis dreamed of earning glory in battle. He got his chance at an early age when he enlisted, along with the other young men of Assisi, to fight in a feud against the neighboring city-state of Perugia. Francis's side lost the battle, and the young romantic was imprisoned. Defeat in battle and illness in prison caused Francis to turn away from his visions of glory on the battlefield.

Francis's path toward God took a series of turns closer and closer to God rather than an all-at-once conversion. However, the course of Francis's life was profoundly changed by at least two formative experiences. On a pilgrimage to Rome, Francis saw a beggar outside of St. Peter's Church. The Holy Spirit moved him to trade places with the beggar. Francis exchanged clothes with the beggar and then spent the day begging for alms. The experience of being poor shook Francis to the core. Later he confronted his own fears of leprosy by hugging a leper. Like trading places with the beggar in Rome, the experience of hugging a leper profoundly changed Francis.

Contrary to the way his story of conversion is often presented, Francis did not change overnight. For years Francis struggled with how to live out the gospel. Shaped by his experiences with the beggar and the leper, he had a strong identification with the poor. Francis eventually cut himself off from the opulent lifestyle of his father and sought a radically simple life. Francis and his followers worked to actually follow Jesus' teaching.

By the time of his death, Francis had accomplished much. Francis's followers became the Order of Friars Minor. The church endorsed the Friars and a similar order was established for women and yet a third for married persons who wanted to keep a rule of simplicity appropriate to them. Thousands of lives were transformed by Francis's response to God's call for deep repentance and radical simplicity.

The progress Francis wanted was for people to follow Jesus, by living out what Jesus taught. The Sermon on the Mount was deeply formative for the friar who had been born into privilege. His purpose was to follow his Lord with no excuses.

Careful research reveals that Francis never wrote the famous saying so often attributed to him. I suspect he never said the phrase either. Yet Francis preached in both word and action: His sermons spoke about a life patterned on Jesus' teachings and his actions illustrated how deeply the gospel had transformed his own life.

We see preaching put into practice by Philip, as he travels to Samaria to proclaim Jesus as the longed-for Messiah. Philip combines words and actions into a transformative testimony as crowds listen eagerly to what he says and then watch carefully as he does signs: "for unclean spirits, crying with loud shrieks, came out of many who were possessed; and many others who were paralyzed or lame were cured."

In these actions, Philip follows the pattern of his Lord. Jesus does not merely preach what it looks like to love one's neighbor in the powerful parable of the Good Samaritan. He enacts that teaching by healing those who cannot even enter the temple courts, including ten lepers at one time (Luke 17:11-19) and a woman suffering from a hemorrhage for twelve years (Matthew 9:20–22, Mark 5:25–34, Luke 8:43–48). Jesus delivers the proclamation that the kingdom of God has come near in both words and actions that reinforce one another.

This same two-fold pattern for proclamation is found within the Baptismal Covenant, which asks, "Will you proclaim by word and example the good news of God in Christ?" The response is, "I will, with God's help."

All Christians are called to use both what we say and what we do to share what God has done for us in Jesus. The Rev. Canon Stephanie Spellers, a leader in the Episcopal Church in reconciliation and evangelism, offers a corrective to the saying: "Preach the gospel at all times. Use words; they're necessary."

If you don't tell someone that the reason you visit with prisoners is because of what Jesus has done for you, how might they connect the two? People of different faiths and those with no religious belief routinely give their time and money to serve the community and those in need. As followers of Jesus, we should not be hesitant to let others know that it is our faith that spurs us to action.

WHAT WE PROCLAIM

While this passage from Acts does not detail what Philip tells the gathered crowd in Samaria, we find in the New Testament the content of what the first Christians say when asked about their faith. Paul puts it succinctly: "We preach Christ crucified." He adds that this proclamation is a stumbling block to Jews and comes across as foolish to others (1 Corinthians 1:23). Preaching Christ crucified means teaching that the promised Jewish Messiah was Jesus, a rabbi crucified by the Romans in a sacrificial death and raised to new life by the power of God. Philip proclaims this message to the eunuch who asks him to explain to him the suffering servant passage from Isaiah. Philip teaches that the Messiah is "Like a sheep...led to the slaughter," before showing how God's love is stronger than death.

To get a sense for what Philip might have said that day in Samaria, read Acts 3:11-26. Here, Peter speaks on Solomon's portico, giving an elevator speech for a crucified and risen Lord to a group gathered in Jerusalem. In Acts 7:2-53, Stephen, a friend of Philip's, gives a fuller account of the faith that is in him.

At the center of the Christian faith stand a manger, a cross, and an empty tomb. The manger where Mary places her newborn baby is a simple feed box in a cave used to stable livestock. People rebel against God, rejecting a relationship with the one who makes us out of love for love. God could stand back as a righteous judge but chooses to enter creation. In his short years of ministry, Jesus lifts up the lowly and loves the unlovable while calling everyone to break down the walls of division that separate us from one another and from God. Jesus enjoys breaking bread with notorious sinners and healing those on the margins, restoring them—and us—to community.

Jesus' words and actions put him at odds with the status quo. Religious and government leaders alike want the rebel rabbi silenced. In emptying himself of his divinity and living among us, Jesus shows the love of God fully. The price of that love is suffering and death on a cross. Jesus chooses to die rather than give up on this love.

Jesus offers his wounds for our healing, his death to give us life, and self-giving love to set us free from the power of evil. This is the life-giving good news at the heart of Christian proclamation.

EXPERIENCE THE GOOD NEWS

The Apostles' and Nicene creeds enumerate what the church has long held true about Jesus, but we should move beyond merely sharing a list of beliefs. G. K. Chesterton, an early twentieth-century theologian, observed that Francis's actions and words were all carried in service to his being in love with Jesus. Chesterton then advised, "Let your religion be less of a theory and more of a love affair."

This is true not just of Francis but also of the earliest Christians. They don't offer courses on evangelism. Instead they hear and believe the good news and then can't contain the joy within them. Like love-struck teens writing the name of their crushes in a notebook, the first believers are consumed by a love for Jesus. They can't help but talk about Jesus. This is because they have experienced Jesus for themselves.

As the same Holy Spirit who inspired the deacon Philip inspires us today, we too can have more than head knowledge about Jesus. We gain heart knowledge through private prayer and public worship, as well as through reading scripture and having the Bible opened up for us in sermons. In these ways and more, we experience Jesus and his proclamation for ourselves.

Such means of grace form us as followers of Jesus and teach us something about how to articulate our faith and how to put our faith into practice. We not only ask God to forgive our sins but also to forgive those who hurt us. As we do this, we begin to move from head knowledge to the heart knowledge of experiencing the free gift of God's grace.

We come to know places, experiences, and people in two ways. I know of the existence of both the Outer Banks of North Carolina and the island of Zanzibar off the coast of Tanzania, but I don't know of them in the same way. I have never visited the Outer Banks, yet I have seen it on maps, I have heard about it from people who visit and live there, and I have seen photos on social media shared by friends while visiting the barrier islands. So I trust there is such a place.

But I know Zanzibar in a different way as I have twice visited the island. I have walked the streets of Old Town and worshiped in the cathedral built on the site of the old slave market—an act of redemption by anti-slavery advocate Dr. David Livingstone. A photo my wife took on one of those visits hangs in our house. It shows me walking with our daughter, Griffin, along a harbor on the Indian Ocean with the distinctive sailboats of the island floating in the background. I know this place because of my experience in it.

The goal of spiritual practices like prayer, Bible study, and worship are to move us from knowing about Jesus in the way I know about the Outer Banks—through others telling me about it—to knowing about Jesus in the way

I know about Zanzibar—through personal experience. And as we have our own experiences of God working in our lives, they become a source of proclamation. We all have moments in our lives when we feel Christ is truly present; when we can articulate that story to ourselves, we can begin to share this life-changing relationship with others.

In fact, the stories of how God has acted in my life are really all I have to share with a friend or co-worker experiencing doubt, pain, or grief. Mostly all I can offer is a listening ear, truly being present with them and hearing their stories. But when we do speak, few of us in those moments recount a story from scripture. Our proclamation is much more personal. What we have to offer, quite humbly, is the way God has been with us in similar times. Something like, "I don't know exactly what you are going through, but I know when my brother died, it was painful. I just kept praying and worshiping, and God gave me peace that is hard to explain. I would never have gotten through it without Jesus."

THE IMPACT OF PROCLAMATION

We expect to find the fruit of the gospel around our congregations, just as scripture expects that when we proclaim the gospel, our words and actions will both oppose evil and bring great joy. What might this look like? Jesus puts it succinctly in the same words of Isaiah that led to the eunuch's conversion, when he reads from the scroll in his home synagogue in Nazareth. His reading declares that he has come to bring good news to the poor, to proclaim release to the captives and recovery of sight to the blind, to let the oppressed go free, and to proclaim that the year of the Lord's favor is fulfilled (Luke 4:18-19). We should expect these same markers to follow the two-fold proclamation of the gospel in our own words and actions.

An example of the power of this proclamation, which the whole world witnessed, came in South Africa. Following the moral leadership of people like Archbishop Desmond Tutu and President Nelson Mandela, the end of apartheid in that nation did not bring a bloodbath, with blacks seeking revenge on whites. Instead, South Africa set up a Truth and Reconciliation Commission, which offered a path to forgiveness and reconciliation. The almost unspeakable evil of apartheid was named clearly, and forgiveness and even sometimes reconciliation were made real. The statements that the government wanted to offer forgiveness and reconciliation where possible were met with concrete steps to embody that ideal in a way that honored victims and did not offer cheap grace to the perpetrators.

The gospel we proclaim continues to change lives for the better. We see people delivered each day from shame to forgiveness, and the power of death is broken each time sinners find the grace to end the cycle of sin. This is why a marker of Christian community is joy, like the great joy experienced in the city of Samaria after they watch friends and family healed and made whole.

FOR REFLECTION AND DISCUSSION

- What in this chapter was challenging or thought provoking?

- When have you seen someone's actions embody the gospel? How did you make the connection between what the person did and the faith behind the deed?

- What experiences in your own life contribute to your experience of God? How have you shared that proclamation with others?

- What would change in your church if everyone became comfortable sharing the gospel through actions and in words?

FOR ACTION

- Create your elevator speech for the gospel. How could you describe to someone in thirty seconds or less why you are a Christian?

- Give your elevator speech to another member of your church and ask for feedback on whether he or she heard the good news of Christ.

CHAPTER 4: LOVING AND SERVING
ADAM TRAMBLEY

I was sitting in the city manager's office.

"The place where things are happening is at the Community and Economic Development Commission," he told me. "Their meeting is at 7:30 a.m. on Tuesday." While my mouth sputtered, "Okay. Thanks," my brain was not happy. I didn't want to be anywhere that early on a Tuesday morning, especially not with a bunch of people I didn't know discussing topics I didn't know much about.

The meeting with the city manager had been prompted by a conversation with my spiritual director a few weeks earlier. I had recently taken a call to serve as a rector in a new community. My spiritual director advised: "Get out and go to some meetings. Find out when the school board meets or something." When I hesitated, he added, "Look, your whole ministry can't be only with the group of people already at your church. Just go. It will be fine."

The next week I called the city manager's office and asked for an appointment. He was thrilled that a new minister in town cared about what was happening in the city. We talked a bit. I asked what he knew about my parish. He said he didn't know anything; people seemed to show up on Sunday and then disappear. I asked how and when I might get involved, and he said, "Tuesday at 7:30 a.m."

In the short time between that meeting and the next Tuesday morning, I had a decision to make. Did I love this community—one I didn't even know yet—enough to wake up early, turn my family's morning routine upside down, and attend a meeting with a bunch of people who I assumed were smart, dedicated, and probably intimidating? No one at the meeting would miss me if I slept in. No one in my parish was holding me accountable to attend, and they might even ask why I showed up at the office later than normal. The only reason to go was because I knew that our parish's relationship with the city couldn't be about just showing up on Sundays and then disappearing. In order for that relationship to change, somebody had to witness to the community that we cared enough to show up on other days.

So I showed up. The next month, I showed up again. And again. And again. Showing up led to more engagement. As people got to know me, they asked me for help with various projects, especially when they learned which gifts I have and which ones I don't. (I'm good at writing newsletter articles and not so good at handling a chainsaw at the neighborhood cleanup.) Eventually I was appointed to the Community and Economic Development Commission, and later I served a term on City Council. This work took time and energy, but the return was amazing. Since I cared enough to work beside them, people felt like our church cared about them and their community—and that God cared, too. They began to see the church not as a tax-free island downtown but as a partner engaged in revitalizing a struggling rust-belt town. We were all trying to make this place a better community together—bankers, small-business owners, young mothers, artists, and the new priest in town. Sometimes they asked for a prayer and sometimes they apologized after they swore, but mostly they came to realize that the church was there for them.

The parish also started being more active in the community. People began to ask about using the facilities for meetings or other activities. When a downtown music store closed, two guitarists started giving lessons at the church (and one week when our organist was on vacation, the city's best blues guitarist was thrilled to play the Sunday services). Pretty soon, the lights in the building were on almost every night, and the parking lot was full. A few people came Sunday morning and became part of the parish's worshiping community, but most importantly the church reclaimed an important place as part of the wider community.

PRAYING FOR THE COMMUNITY

Starting with that early morning meeting, our commitment as a congregation to love and serve the community required intention and action. First, we prayed more for the community, both as individuals and as a church. Second, flowing out of prayer, was a willingness to sacrifice in order to love and serve our community. Praying for our community is an essential element of loving and serving; prayer develops and expands our capacity for love and makes our service more effective. Our prayers for the community can take many forms, but without engaging in prayer, we can't hope to see great joy come to our cities.

One of the sweetest fruits of prayer is being granted the grace to see our communities from God's perspective. When we hold the people, the neighborhoods, the businesses, the schools, and the public servants in our communities up to the throne of God, the cataracts in our own spiritual vision are removed. As we ask God to be at work in the troubled sections of town and offer thanks for places where healthy development is occurring, we gain an increased sense of God's call and mission for our area. The act of lifting our city's conflicts and tragedies to the heavenly mercy seat offers us a glimpse into the compassion and love God has for all people. Asking God's blessing on the schools and day-care centers opens to us the vistas of the divine potential and possibility in even the most depressed region.

Prayer connects us with our communities in profound ways. The very act of praying is an act of love. As we pray for the cities and communities we live in, we carve channels of love in our own hearts for the people and places around us. Through our intercessions, we walk with others into the courts of heaven and that journey creates a stronger, more loving bond between us. The love that pours out of our hearts in prayer begins to move in other ways as well. Prayer is the preparation we need in our churches to do the difficult work of loving and serving our communities.

Of course, prayer is also effective in and of itself. Asking God to bless our communities is probably the single most loving thing we can do for them. In prayer, we ask God to do God's part in bringing great joy to our communities, and when we pray passionately and lovingly, we also offer ourselves to God to be used for God's good work.

Practically, those who pray regularly for their communities engage in a number of types of prayer. First, and probably most important, is to pray as individuals for the needs we see in the community. For some people, this kind of prayer happens during their regular prayer time. The needs encountered in the city are added to the intercessions offered for themselves, their families, and their church. Some people stop and offer prayer immediately when they encounter these needs, whether those are the personal requests of a community leader, an empty storefront waiting to be filled, or a taskforce trying to reduce opioid abuse. However and wherever our intentions are offered, the most important thing is that we begin praying.

Once individuals begin praying, they can bring their prayers to the wider church. Specific requests can be given to church prayer groups and prayer chains. The Prayers of the People in worship can and should include the needs and concerns of the surrounding community. Various people at my church have written specific Prayers of the People each week to incorporate local tragedies, celebration of local events, and asking for God's blessing on particular initiatives. We spent a few years with a prayer cycle of groups in the community that we wanted to pray for: teachers; doctors, nurses, medical professionals; small business owners; mill workers; police, fire, and other first responders; and bankers and financial services professionals. Such prayers ensure the church remains connected to the community.

Prayerwalking can also be a powerful way both to pray and love the community. Prayerwalking is not difficult, and many people find it invigorating and fun (some have even used it to help them lose weight). I often prayerwalk by myself but going with a partner or as a team is even better. All that is required for prayerwalking is a willingness to take a thirty- to sixty-minute walk in the community or neighborhood and to be in conversation with God about what you see. As you encounter places where things are going well, give thanks. Where you see problems, ask God to intervene. When you find the beginnings of new life, ask God's blessing. The more you walk and pray, the more you will see in the community and what you see will draw you deeper into prayer.

Some who pray regularly for cities suggest a focus on five aspects: spiritual, government, education, business, and media. These sectors are key in any community, and they can always use our prayers.

SACRIFICING FOR THE COMMUNITY

Our prayer for the community prepares us to love our community. Loving our community leads to serving it and serving always involves some element of sacrifice.

Healthy, thriving churches go out into the community and meet its needs. These might not always be the needs that are easiest for the church to meet. In Acts 8, Philip presumably has experience with feeding ministries. But the city of Samaria doesn't need a feeding program. He could have taken some loaves and fishes and given the city dinner that night, but instead, the city needs to have unclean spirits cast out and the sick healed. So that's what Philip does. Great joy comes to the city because Philip loves them enough to do what they need. Great joy will come to our cities when we do the same.

One of the differences between thriving and dying churches is the way they each approach their community. Many dying churches see the people around them as potential sources of support to the congregation in doing what it has always done. Fundraisers are held for the church operating budget, so money flows from the community into the church. New people are sought to fill committee positions vacated only when veteran members become too old to continue. Children and youth are invited to Sunday school and education programs that haven't changed significantly in decades. The building is only open for use by those who attend the church, not for community or organizational gatherings. These types of churches love themselves more than the communities around them.

Loving, thriving churches see themselves as being called to give away their resources to meet the needs of the community, confident that God will provide what is needed to do the work God is calling them to. Loving churches give space to groups during the week that need a place to hold a meeting. Loving churches give time to neighbors who show up with some sort of need. Loving churches give money away to programs that help foster change in their communities.

Chapter 8 of this book explores concrete ways to learn about the needs of the community. But we also learn about these needs simply by being in relationship with those in our community. As we encounter those around us, we usually find specific ways that we can love and serve them. Depending on an area's needs and the church's gifts, congregations can offer food pantries, daycare centers, afterschool programs, recovery programs, job-training classes, scout troops, arts and music centers, and other types of programming. Church members may volunteer as individuals or in groups at local schools, senior centers, community centers, or other nonprofits. The church doesn't have to tackle every community problem, and it will not turn a community around overnight. Loving churches identify the particular needs of a particular group and do whatever they can to meet those needs.

Meeting these community needs will change individuals and congregations. As walls are broken down, the congregation's priorities change. Instead of only caring about people who are already part of the church, the congregation cares also about this new group of people being served. However we define formal congregational membership, these new people we come to love and serve in our cities become a real part of the community.

When Philip brings the good news to the Samaritans, suddenly Samaritan life plays a larger role in the wider church. Samaritan needs, hopes, dreams, and particularly Samaritan insights about God all become a part of the growing Body of Christ.

The early church, spurred on by Philip, uses its gifts to love and serve the Samaritans, and great joy comes to that city. The church today, represented by each of us, can use our gifts to love and serve our own communities, and great joy will come to our cities as well. All it takes is prayer, sacrifice…and occasionally getting up early on Tuesday mornings.

FOR REFLECTION AND DISCUSSION

- What struck you most in this discussion of loving and serving the community?

- How do you and your congregation pray for your community? What difference might it make if everyone in your church prayed regularly for the community?

- How do you and your congregation show your love for your community?

- What steps are you willing to take to love people in your community that you haven't met yet?

FOR ACTION

- Write a prayer for a community need this week. Share this prayer with others and ask to include it in your Sunday worship.

- Pick one of the five centers for community prayer (spiritual, government, education, business, and media), and pray for that area every day for a week. Share your experience of this kind of prayer with others.

- Organize a prayerwalk in the neighborhood around your church. Give God thanks for the good you see. Ask God to bless places that could use a boost, and to intervene where necessary. Spend some time after the walk to share what you noticed with your companions.

SECTION 3
ACTS 8:9-25

Now a certain man named Simon had previously practiced magic in the city and amazed the people of Samaria, saying that he was someone great. All of them, from the least to the greatest, listened to him eagerly, saying, "This man is the power of God that is called Great." And they listened eagerly to him because for a long time he had amazed them with his magic. But when they believed Philip, who was proclaiming the good news about the kingdom of God and the name of Jesus

Christ, they were baptized, both men and women. Even Simon himself believed. After being baptized, he stayed constantly with Philip and was amazed when he saw the signs and great miracles that took place.

Now when the apostles at Jerusalem heard that Samaria had accepted the word of God, they sent Peter and John to them. The two went down and prayed for them that they might receive the Holy Spirit (for as yet the Spirit had not come upon any of them; they had only been baptized in the name of the Lord Jesus). Then Peter and John laid their hands on them, and they received the Holy Spirit. Now when Simon saw that the Spirit was given through the laying on of the apostles' hands, he offered them money, saying, "Give me also this power so that anyone on whom I lay my hands may receive the Holy Spirit." But Peter said to him, "May your silver perish with you, because you thought you could obtain God's gift with money! You have no part or share in this, for your heart is not right before God. Repent therefore of this wickedness of yours, and pray to the Lord that, if possible, the intent of your heart may be forgiven you. For I see that you are in the gall of bitterness and the chains of wickedness." Simon answered, "Pray for me to the Lord, that nothing of what you have said may happen to me."

Now after Peter and John had testified and spoken the word of the Lord, they returned to Jerusalem, proclaiming the good news to many villages of the Samaritans.

THE STORY
BRENDAN O'SULLIVAN-HALE
HOLLI POWELL

Tradition has not been kind to Simon Magus, also known as Simon the Magician or Simon the Sorcerer. Not only does he have a sin named after him ("simony," the attempt to purchase religious authority, status, or even salvation), but some Christian historians even refer to him as the Father of All Heresy. In myths perpetuated by church historiographers Justin Martyr and Irenaeus, Simon is cast out by the apostles and moves on to Rome, where he claims to be the reincarnated Jesus, performs "miracles," and welcomes followers. Legend says that Simon is levitating before his followers when both Peter and Paul kneel to pray, and the power of their prayers brings Simon crashing to earth and to his death. In fact, there's even a church in Rome, Santa Francesca Romana, that claims to have been built on the spot where Simon fell and to have a marble slab with dents where Peter and Paul's knees hit the ground. Simon's story is the subject of several novels, movies, and operas, and in Dante's *Inferno*, he appears in the eighth circle of hell.

The legends of Simon's deeds are lurid, but they reflect a genuine ambiguity in Acts about the sincerity of his conversion. The text plainly states that "even Simon himself believed," but the circumstances that led to his conversion imply motivations besides a change of heart. When Philip comes to town, proclaiming Jesus as the Messiah and performing healings and exorcisms in his name, great joy comes to the city. But that joy immediately threatens Simon's status as "the power of God that is called Great." Whatever Simon's sincerity, his conversion is an example of the gift of faith as seed that falls on rocky soil (Matthew 13:20-21).

Meanwhile, the apostles in Jerusalem hear that the Samaritans have converted. They send Peter and John to visit, in what seems strangely like a modern Episcopal bishop making the rounds of churches for confirmations. When Peter and John lay their hands on the Samaritan believers, the Holy Spirit comes upon them, and Simon sees an opportunity. He asks Peter and John if he too can possess the power to bestow the Holy Spirit; Simon even offers to pay for the privilege—hence the sin of simony named in his dishonor. Even though Simon has accepted Jesus, he hasn't given up his desire to be the One Who Amazes. We scoff at Simon, but we might do well to wonder: Is Simon's offer so different from ours? Believing in Jesus doesn't automatically erase our egos (though it would be great if it did), and it doesn't magically change our ways of doing things. Simon has spent his life gaining power and prestige by doing extraordinary things, and in a moment of weakness, he goes back to old, familiar habits.

Peter doesn't see Simon as a new believer with much to learn about following Jesus. Rather, Peter sees Simon as a false prophet attempting to bend God's will to his own in order to gain money and power. And Peter responds accordingly—harshly rejecting Simon's attempt to buy God's favor from the apostles. Peter points Simon toward what God truly desires: not a transactional relationship but the sacrifice of a "broken and contrite heart" (Psalm 51:17). God doesn't want our money, *per se*; God wants our egos, our pride, and all the parts of our selves and lives that separate us from the Divine.

The text leaves unclear what happens to Simon, though legend assumes the worst. Peter instructs Simon to pray for God's forgiveness, but Simon asks Peter to pray for him instead. Simon may or may not follow the path Peter offers him, but for us in our own struggles to remain faithful, Peter draws a clear map. We cannot heal our own hearts: Only God can do that. Prayer and repentance are the ways to bring our hearts closer to God's desire for us.

CHAPTER 5: REPENTANCE
SUSAN BROWN SNOOK

At first glance, the story of Simon Magus seems very odd to modern readers. It assumes Simon can do powerful acts of magic, violating the laws of nature. Simon's magic tricks are amazing enough that the people of Samaria call him "the power of God that is called great." As twenty-first-century Christians, we are likely skeptical about Simon's magical abilities, which may lead us to write off this story altogether. But magic is not the point of the story. Luke shows us that Simon's earthly power of magic, whatever it is, cannot stand against the power of the Holy Spirit—the main character of the Book of Acts—whose work is powerfully and astoundingly made manifest throughout Luke's writing.

Once we look past our skepticism of his magic tricks, we can see Simon Magus as a profoundly human character. When we read the Bible, it is often easy to fit the characters into mental schemes of good guys vs. bad guys. We easily categorize the Bible characters this way: disciples on one side, Pharisees on the other. People whom Jesus heals and feeds on one side, Roman soldiers on the other. Simple, right? And of course, we assume that if we had been there, we would stand with the good folks, following and learning from Jesus and not succumbing to the grievous mistakes made by so

many other folks in the stories. We love Jesus, after all—
we're the good guys.

We do the same in the present world, assuming people
are either all bad or all good (and of course, we're on the
good side!). We disagree with someone and write them
off as not worth our effort. We dislike the stance of a
political party and believe all its followers are evil. We are
suspicious of people who look, think, or act differently
than we do. We classify the world into "us" and "them."

Yet Simon doesn't fit quite so easily into this good vs.
evil scheme. If we think about his story carefully, Simon
actually calls the whole framework into question. He is
partly good and partly bad. He sees the power of the Holy
Spirit and immediately recognizes it as a power greater
than his own. In his astonishment, he wants what he sees
others receiving. He's an admirer of the true God—he
recognizes God, he believes, and he is baptized.

On the other hand, Simon is an imperfect Christian at best.
He wants the Spirit's power to increase his own power,
and he is willing to pay well to receive it. He assumes the
Spirit is a commodity to be bought and sold. He desires
the power of the Spirit, yet he is profoundly misguided
in how to acquire it. He mistakes the ways of the Spirit
for the ways of the world. Simon is deeply human, a mix
of good impulses and wrong actions, a heart that desires
to be faithful combined with a deeply erroneous way of
going about it. Sound familiar? We know many people
like Simon.

And, if we are honest, we will admit that we are a little like Simon ourselves. We aren't all good, and we aren't all bad; we are a mix of motives and impulses. We do our best, but sometimes we fail. At times we set our self-regard aside and act in inspiringly generous, self-giving, Christ-like ways. But we are also deeply selfish. We try to see the world God's way but often look through the blinders of self-interest. We think we are doing the right things, asking for the right things, and then, like Simon, we are brought up short with the realization that we have been going about it all wrong. We believe we are following Jesus, but it turns out we've been following ourselves instead.

It's hard to fit real people like ourselves into simple categories of good and bad. We live in an imperfect world, and we are all tempted by its values. Luke shows us that there is no contest between earthly magic and the work of the Spirit. Further, these words from Luke reveal to us that humans who try to operate under an earthly set of rules will fail miserably at opening themselves up to the gifts of the Spirit. We are citizens of God's heavenly kingdom, while at the same time we are constantly tempted to give our allegiance to a sin-filled world.

Simon's rebuke from Peter is harsh: "May your silver perish with you, because you thought you could obtain God's gift with money! You have no part or share in this, for your heart is not right before God. Repent therefore of this wickedness of yours, and pray to the Lord that, if possible, the intent of your heart may be forgiven you.

For I see that you are in the gall of bitterness and the chains of wickedness."

Yet Simon is not beyond help. His reply to Peter is humble: "Pray for me to the Lord, that nothing of what you have said may happen to me." I hope that I could respond with such openness to such a rebuke. Luke doesn't tell us what happens to Simon, but I pray he accepted Peter's invitation to repent.

REPENT?

There's that word: *repent*. This word isn't exactly at the height of popularity in our feel-good world. It's a word that conjures up pictures of sweaty televangelists and sign-carrying street-corner preachers, a word that threatens our carefully nurtured yet fragile self-esteem. No, repent is not a popular word.

Yet it's a word that is pivotal to the biblical witness about our relationship to Jesus. In the Gospel of Mark, Jesus' central message is about repentance: "The time is fulfilled, and the kingdom of God has come near; repent, and believe in the good news" (Mark 1:15). In Luke, the resurrected Jesus declares that proclaiming repentance is the mission of the church, saying "repentance and forgiveness of sins is to be proclaimed in his name to all nations, beginning from Jerusalem" (Luke 24:47). On the day of Pentecost, Peter proclaims that repentance is the first task of new believers in Christ: "Repent, and be baptized every one of you in the name of Jesus Christ so that your sins may be forgiven; and you will receive the gift of the Holy Spirit" (Acts 2:38). Repentance is not a step to be skipped or ignored; it is fundamental to the Christian life.

What does it mean to repent? As a young person, I attended several evangelical tent revivals. Each featured dramatic speakers telling their crisis-ridden life stories— drug use, prison terms, gang membership. We listeners held our breath and sat on the edge of our seats as we heard how their lives had been dramatically turned around by the power of Christ. I never doubted their witness or the miracles Christ had worked in their lives, but in some perverse way, their stories reinforced my own sense of self-righteousness. I had never been involved in a crisis-ridden, crime-filled life. What did I need to be saved from?

It took years to realize that my sins were probably much closer to those of Simon Magus than to the individuals at the dramatic tent revivals of my youth. I lived a respectable life, making a name for myself in my profession. I hadn't done much that the world would recognize as wrong. I attended church from time to time and called myself a Christian. Yet I was devoting my life to pursuing my own desires rather than opening myself to God's desires for me. Realizing this error was my first step to repentance.

I think many Christians are in a similar place. We live as good citizens; most of our sins aren't identifiable or dramatic. They are inward. They are attitudes of the heart, desires that conform to the desires of the world. And these desires of the world are not so different now than they were in Simon's time. The world entices us to desire what Simon desires: fame, success, power, money. There are other idols too: beauty, sex, celebrity, fame. The world makes idols of these pursuits and tempts us to worship them instead of God, to make the quest of our desires first priority in our lives. The world invites us to put ourselves before others and work for our own success. In other words, the world continues to tempt us with the very same temptation the serpent laid before Adam and Eve: "You will be like God" (Genesis 3:5). Idolatry is the original sin, and it's not so unusual: Jesus is also tempted to worship an idol (Matthew 4:8-10).

Christian faith calls us to set these desires aside and worship God alone. That's what repentance is. It is having a new mind and a new heart. It's making a decision to follow Jesus even when we want only to follow ourselves. It's a lifelong resistance to the powers of idolatry that call us to worship ourselves and follow the false idols of this world. Repentance is a willingness to let God take our open hearts and mold them to God's purposes. And yes, we will fail, but when we open our eyes to God's way of seeing the world, we will have the courage to try and try again, devoting ourselves to following Jesus instead of ourselves.

Repentance is the process by which God opens our eyes to a new way of thinking, living, and being. Repentance is what Paul describes in the letter to the Romans: "Do not be conformed to this world, but be transformed by the renewing of your minds, so that you may discern what is the will of God—what is good and acceptable and perfect" (Romans 12:2).

Repentance is a new attitude, a new mind. That's what *metanoia*, an ancient Greek word that is commonly translated as repentance, means. In our modern world, we think of repentance as breast-beating guilt. But in the New Testament, repentance—*metanoia*—means being given a "mind from above," a new mind, a new way of looking at the world. It is a turnaround, a readjustment of our values and priorities. It is a way of asking God to work through us, rather than our trying to use God's power for our own purposes as Simon did. Repentance is a new start in life, a start we sometimes need to ask God to give us every day. Repentance is not guilt at all but the release from guilt.

In the Episcopal service of Holy Eucharist, we often begin with the Collect for Purity:

> Almighty God, to you all hearts are open, all desires known, and from you no secrets are hid: Cleanse the thoughts of our hearts by the inspiration of your Holy Spirit, that we may perfectly love you, and worthily magnify your holy Name; through Christ our Lord. *Amen.* (*The Book of Common Prayer*)

This beautiful prayer, with its echoes of Psalm 51 ("Create in me a clean heart, O God, and renew a right spirit within me"), reminds us that God already knows our hearts and minds. Repentance is our acknowledgement that God still loves us! And it means we are willing to accept the cleansing and renewal that God offers.

Confession and absolution are offered in the celebration of Episcopal eucharist, so we can ask God to cleanse our hearts before receiving Jesus' gift of himself in bread and wine. I like to take some silent time before saying the confession, to bring my whole self before God. But the General Confession in worship does not require us to list all our sins, to concentrate deeply on feeling remorseful, or to experience relief. It simply asks us to bring ourselves before God and acknowledge that we have not loved God with our whole hearts or our neighbor as ourselves. The work of forgiveness is God's. The ministry of redemption has already been performed by Jesus; the gift of reconciliation comes to us through the Holy Spirit. Each time we accept these gifts, we give ourselves the opportunity to begin life anew.

If we want more in-depth discussion of confession and forgiveness, counseling about how to make amends for the wrongs we have done, or the simple, personal assurance that God has forgiven us—yes, even us— then private confession with a priest is available in the Episcopal Church. Confession is not designed to make us feel guilty. Rather, confession can relieve us of guilt and assures us that our sins are erased and that God loves us passionately and eternally.

After all, forgiveness is God's job, not ours. We simply have to open our hearts and allow God to do the rest. Reminding ourselves of the forgiveness God has already offered us in Jesus is a comfort to us and opens our hearts and minds to accept God's gift.

The more difficult part of confession and repentance is dedicating ourselves to living differently after we are forgiven. This means opening our hearts to God through prayer, worship, Bible study, and service—the things we talk about in this book. Living a repentant life means understanding that our own instincts and desires are not always the same as God's. It means asking sincerely how the Holy Spirit is leading us and following where the Spirit leads.

Simon's mistake isn't magic. He recognizes its paltry power when compared with the power of the Holy Spirit. Simon's mistake is trying to fit the Holy Spirit into the values of the world he lives in, a world where money and power reign supreme. Repentance means opening our eyes to a new world, where only God is supreme, and we can gladly and willingly accept the gifts of the Spirit.

FOR REFLECTION AND DISCUSSION

- What comes to mind when you hear the word repentance? Did the discussion in this chapter give you new ways of looking at what it means to repent?

- When in your life or in the lives of those around you have you observed people living in obedience to one of the idols of this world? What is the role of the church in helping people turn away from false idols and follow the living God instead?

- The Penitential Order in *The Book of Common Prayer*, pages 351-352, contains three quotes from scripture about repentance:

  Jesus said, "The first commandment is this: Hear, O Israel: The Lord our God is the only Lord. Love the Lord your God with all your heart, with all your soul, with all your mind, and with all your strength. The second is this: Love your neighbor as yourself. There is no other commandment greater than these." *Mark 12:29-31*

  If we say that we have no sin, we deceive ourselves, and the truth is not in us. But if we confess our sins, God, who is faithful and just, will forgive our sins and cleanse us from all unrighteousness. *1 John 1:8, 9*

  Since we have a great high priest who has passed through the heavens, Jesus, the Son of God, let us with confidence draw near to the throne of grace, that we may receive mercy and find grace to help in time of need. *Hebrews 4:14, 16*

- As you read these scripture verses, which of them brings you comfort? Which of them challenges you to see your faith in a new way? Which of them asks you to live a new life?

- In the passage from Acts 8, Simon Magus tries to buy something that the apostles could not sell, and they rebuke him. When have you seen people ask the church to provide something that was inappropriate for the church to give? How should the church respond to such situations?

FOR ACTION

- Read the Parable of the Loving Father in Luke 15:11-32 (sometimes called the Parable of the Prodigal Son). When have you felt like the younger brother who squandered much of his life? When have you felt like the older brother who did almost everything right? When have you felt like a loving father just waiting to welcome someone home? What insight does this story give you into God's forgiveness for us?

- If you are so inclined, schedule a private appointment with a priest to pray through the Reconciliation of a Penitent service (confession) together and receive the priest's counseling and absolution.

CHAPTER 6: PRAYER
ADAM TRAMBLEY

When was the last time someone came to your church and offered you money for the ability to pray the way you pray? I can't remember either.

Not long ago, I received a phone call. The caller had come by the church a few weeks earlier with a financial need. We talked. I listened. I asked if we could pray and we did. The room grew quiet. The atmosphere felt rich. Tears were shed. Through the church's discretionary fund, I was able to provide a small amount of financial assistance, which seemed like the right thing to do. I didn't hear anything from this person for a few weeks, then the phone rang, and I recognized the voice. I immediately began to think about my discretionary fund balance and whether I could, or should, help again. The caller described a new difficulty in some detail. Then the twist came. "Pastor, I know you helped me before, but can you pray for me and this need now?" Prayer was more important than the money. We prayed. Then the person thanked me and hung up.

In this section of Acts 8, Simon Magus is called great for a reason. Like others throughout history who have been called great, Simon knows what is important. He intuits immediately that the Holy Spirit is more valuable than his magic—or his money. He offers what he owns in exchange for the ability to transform people's lives. Simon is absolutely right in valuing above all else the incredible gift of praying for people to receive the Holy Spirit. Yet, Simon is absolutely wrong about how this gift actually works.

What Simon doesn't understand is that neither prayer nor the Holy Spirit's presence comes in a transactional economy. The power of the Holy Spirit isn't for sale and is not guaranteed by doing certain things in certain ways. Simon's magic may work in this way—but not the Holy Spirit. The Holy Spirit descends through the prayers of people who have a relationship with Jesus Christ, and it descends upon people who want to deepen that relationship. Simon is not looking for repentance or relationship. He is looking for a better source of magic. Needless to say, Peter is not impressed.

As a church, we are called to be like Simon Magus in recognizing the unsurpassed value of prayer, particularly of praying for the presence of the Holy Spirit. But we are also called to be bolder than Simon and more vulnerable and to recognize that this pearl of great price leads us into a deeper relationship with God, one focused on repentance, obedience, and prayer.

PRAYING FOR THE HOLY SPIRIT

Simon sees Peter and John praying for people and laying hands on them so that they receive the Holy Spirit. Simon wants to buy this ability. Perhaps we, like Simon, would like this ability to call upon the Holy Spirit and be answered at our direction. Yet, pinning down the Holy Spirit is not possible. At various times and places, different churches and denominations have had various interpretations about the best ways to envoke the presence of the Holy Spirit and to recognize that presence. The good news is that most, if not all, of those earnest understandings have resulted in transformed lives and communities.

One way that the Holy Spirit is prayed for occurs during the rite of confirmation. In the Episcopal Church and some other denominations, a bishop lays hands on a person who is making a mature profession of faith. Another tradition practiced in some denominations is the "baptism of the Holy Spirit," which is often accompanied by speaking in tongues and other expressions of the Spirit. In the Acts 8 passage, we are not told exactly what Simon sees, but he surely witnesses some kind of miraculous manifestation of the Spirit's presence as Peter and John pray. Otherwise Simon would not offer all his silver in exchange for receiving the Holy Spirit!

Regardless of the different ways people receive the Holy Spirit, there is a common, consistent outcome: People's lives are changed.

The presence of the Holy Spirit manifests the fruits of the Spirit. These fruits, expressed in Paul's letter to the Galatians, are love, joy, peace, patience, kindness, generosity, faithfulness, gentleness, and self-control. Imagine the scene Simon witnesses as these fruits are exhibited in the lives of new believers. Imagine the change in someone who deeply feels God's love, maybe after a lifetime of exclusion. Imagine the laughter bubbling out of someone who has experienced the Spirit's joy in the midst of physical, emotional, or spiritual pain. Imagine peace infusing a congregation of Samaritans, people in the middle of all sorts of ethnic and religious conflicts. The fruits of the Spirit are transformative—and certainly worth at least a lifetime's supply of silver.

Yet these fruits aren't the only results of the presence of the Spirit in a person's life. The Holy Spirit also unlocks a person's individual spiritual gifts. After Peter and John pray for someone, that person may now be able to speak in tongues or offer prophecy. Simon might have also seen the Holy Spirit's gifts used for healing or administration or teaching or evangelism. Those who have the apostles' hands laid upon them find new purpose and energy, and their efforts bear good fruit. Simon surely experiences the power of the Holy Spirit not as a one-hit wonder but as the deep, penetrating rhythm that undergirds a believer's life.

Unfortunately Simon seems to have missed other equally important, but less obvious, results of the Holy Spirit's presence. Above all else, the Spirit lets us know ourselves as adopted children of God. Romans 8:16 says "it is that very Spirit bearing witness with our spirit that we are children of God."

Everything else the Holy Spirit does draws us more deeply into the fullness of our relationship as children of God. The Spirit lets us understand that we are joint heirs with Christ in the fullness of the reign of God, and the Spirit provides what we need to live into this incredible calling.

The Holy Spirit also convicts us of sin. As we come to know the presence of the Holy Spirit within us, we become more aware of the places in our lives where we have been shutting God out. We cannot maintain a closeness to God and undertake activities that are disobedient to God or hurt ourselves or others. The light of God, shining in our hearts through the Spirit, helps us see where we need to repent and make different choices. When we fail to repent, we lose the fullness of the fruits of the Spirit. The presence of the Holy Spirit is such a gift that we become acutely aware when we start to lose it, and we want to do everything in our power to make sure we don't lose it again! Unfortunately, Simon never seems to receive the deep relationship with God that comes through the presence of the Holy Spirit, and he does not recognize the great sin he proposes to Peter.

The presence of the Holy Spirit is the foundation of everything good and effective that we do as a church community. Part of our core work as individuals and as a faith community is to pray for the Holy Spirit to come into our lives and the lives of the members of the Body of Christ. Our prayers for the Holy Spirit's presence should not stop with our fellow members. We should pray to experience the fruits of the Holy Spirit in our communities, our cities, our schools, and other organizations. We can also pray for the Holy Spirit to be present and at work in the midst of the relationships and situations in our lives. We pray to know the love of the Holy Spirit in our families, the peace of the Holy Spirit in our work places, and the joy of the Holy Spirit in our social events. The prayers of the church for the Holy Spirit's presence, in whatever form, are extremely important.

WOOING THE HOLY SPIRIT

Once we recognize that we need to pray for the Holy Spirit, the question of how to offer that prayer remains. This passage of Acts is clear that we can't buy the privilege of having the third person of the Trinity materialize. The believers in Samaria call for Peter and John to come and pray. What can we do today to invite the Holy Spirit into our hearts and lives?

One prayerful priest I know talks about "wooing" the Holy Spirit. The Holy Spirit doesn't show up because we hold the right worship services or say the right words. The Holy Spirit shows up because people who have created space in their lives for God to inhabit lovingly invite the Holy Spirit to come into other places that are yearning for that same transforming presence. Peter and John have a closeness to Jesus Christ and to the Holy Spirit, and they bring that presence to the Samaritans who are preparing similar places in their lives.

Once we have prepared a place for the Holy Spirit in our lives, then we focus on strengthening and deepening our relationship with God so that the Holy Spirit can work through us. Preparing a place occurs through repentance; the work of relationship happens through obedience and prayer.

The previous chapter explored repentance in depth, but at a fundamental level, we need to acknowledge that the Holy Spirit will not enter our lives if we close the door to God through sin. Either we repent of our sins and try to live righteous and godly lives, or we live for ourselves alone and let God know that we aren't interested.

Without repentance and amendment of life, we haven't prepared a home for the Holy Spirit to inhabit. When the Samaritans are baptized, most of them have the experience of repenting and turning away from their old lives. Simon wants to keep his old life but with a more powerful Christian sheen. When Peter and John come, the Holy Spirit descends on many of the Samaritans but not on Simon. True repentance is necessary.

Obedience goes hand in hand with repentance. By being obedient to what God wants for us, we take care to avoid actions that will push out the Holy Spirit. We try to align our thoughts and actions with God's desires and purposes for our lives. Love of God and neighbor becomes more important to us than our own comfort and convenience. We want to walk in God's ways and not stumble along our own paths.

Along with obedience is the ongoing work of deepening our relationship and continually offering ourselves to God. This work is the regular, exhilarating, dutiful, joyful act of prayer. The goal of our life of prayer is to be fully transparent with God. We desire God's desire for us. We want what God wants for us. Our spirit dances continually with the Holy Spirit. As Saint Paul says, it is no longer I, but Christ who lives within me.

Entering deeply into a divine union with God does not demand a certain formula of prayer or a particular set of disciplines. But we do need to develop a healthy and dynamic prayer life and undertake spiritual disciplines appropriate to our own personalities and gifts. Wise people have found the following components helpful:

- Joining with the Body of Christ for corporate worship at least weekly

- Experiencing a daily encounter with God in scripture, through the Daily Office, some other Bible reading schedule, or a practice of *lectio divina*

- Setting aside daily or regular time before God in silent contemplation, which could include centering prayer, praying with icons, or being in nature

- Offering daily intercessory prayers for your needs and for your loved ones, the church, and the world

- Fasting from food for a particular period as a powerful form of intercessory prayer and as a way to pray with your whole body while strengthening your ability to say no to yourself

- Taking time to stop and evaluate where you are in your walk with God through spiritual direction, confession, spiritual friendships, retreats, pilgrimages, or other times of discussion with wise spiritual counselors

When our life of prayer matures into a deep relationship with God, the Holy Spirit is so much a part of our lives that we cannot imagine being without this presence. Peter and John are so close to God that when they show up in Samaria, the Holy Spirit comes with them. When they pray for the Holy Spirit to fill the new believers, the Holy Spirit shows up.

Simon is willing to pay big money for the opportunity to call upon the Holy Spirit with confidence. We don't need to pay with big money. Instead, we pay with our lives. We give our hearts in love, our wills in obedience, and our spirits in prayer. We prefer nothing over Christ and take up our crosses to follow him.

When we are filled with the Holy Spirit, amazing things happen. We see the kind of transformation in our lives and in our churches that we read about in Acts. People are attracted to what is happening in our communities, and they come to believe and enter into relationship with Jesus. Members of the Body of Christ use their spiritual gifts powerfully to build each other up and to reach unbelievers. We find great joy in our cities, along with great love, profound peace, and all of the fruits of the Spirit.

Simon recognizes the value of this power, but he can't obtain it. We can have it freely, but too often we undervalue it. Certainly, the Holy Spirit can show up and do amazing things without us. Yet God calls us to pray for the presence of the Holy Spirit in our lives, homes, churches, and cities. In doing so, we build the foundation for ministry empowered by the Holy Spirit.

FOR REFLECTION AND DISCUSSION

- What most interests you in this discussion about praying for the Holy Spirit?

- Where do you see the fruits of the Spirit present in your life and your congregation?

- What ways might you more intentionally woo the Holy Spirit in your life?

- What would your church look like if everyone regularly made time to be present with the Holy Spirit in prayer?

FOR ACTION

- Join with two or three faithful friends and pray for God to send the Holy Spirit to fill your hearts, your churches, and your communities.

- Approach people in your church who pray regularly. Ask them about their experience of the Holy Spirit.

- Join one of the active prayer ministries in your congregation.

SECTION FOUR
ACTS 8:26-40

Then an angel of the Lord said to Philip, "Get up and go toward the south to the road that goes down from Jerusalem to Gaza." (This is a wilderness road.) So he got up and went. Now there was an Ethiopian eunuch, a court official of the Candace, queen of the Ethiopians, in charge of her entire treasury. He had come to Jerusalem to worship and was returning home; seated in his chariot, he was reading the prophet Isaiah. Then the Spirit said to Philip, "Go over to this chariot and join it." So Philip ran up to it and heard him reading the prophet Isaiah. He asked, "Do you understand what you are reading?" He replied, "How can I, unless someone guides me?" And he invited Philip to get in and sit beside him. Now the passage of the scripture that he was reading was this:

> *"Like a sheep he was led to the slaughter,*
> *And like a lamb silent before its shearer,*
> *So he does not open his mouth.*
> *In his humiliation justice was denied him.*
> *Who can describe his generation?*
> *For his life is taken away from the earth."*

The eunuch asked Philip, "About whom, may I ask you, does the prophet say this, about himself or about someone else?" Then Philip began to speak, and starting with this scripture, he proclaimed to him the good news about Jesus. As they were going along the road, they came to some water; and the eunuch said, "Look, here is water! What is to prevent me from being baptized?" He commanded the chariot to stop, and both of them, Philip and the eunuch, went down into the water, and Philip baptized him. When they came up out of the water, the Spirit of the Lord snatched Philip away; the eunuch saw him no more, and went on his way rejoicing. But Philip found himself at Azotus, and as he was passing through the region, he proclaimed the good news to all the towns until he came to Caesarea.

THE STORY
BRENDAN O'SULLIVAN-HALE
HOLLI POWELL

An angel of the Lord tells Philip to get up and go, and Philip does. No matter that the wilderness road to Gaza isn't likely to lead him to any converts or crowds like the ones he preached to in Samaria, or any flashy miracles. Philip hears the voice of the angel of God clearly, and he obeys.

He obeys a second time when, on his journey, he encounters a stranger sitting in his chariot. All Philip is able to tell from his initial view is that the stranger is from a different race and a different socioeconomic class. This could be a dangerous situation for Philip, or at the very least, an uncomfortable one. But the Spirit of God tells Philip to approach the chariot, and Philip literally runs to obey.

As he approachs the chariot, he hears the Ethiopian eunuch, a court official in charge of his queen's treasury, reading aloud from the Book of Isaiah. The Acts passage doesn't tell us if Philip hesitates or wonders about the advisability of what comes next, but we can only imagine how we might respond in Philip's stead. But Philip steps away from comfort and toward the urging of the Holy

Spirit, asking the Ethiopian if he understands what he is reading.

This is a direct and impertinent question under virtually any circumstance, but the Ethiopian's response shows it to be the right one. "How can I, unless someone guides me?" The Ethiopian isn't named in this story, but his name is less important than the descriptors we are given for him. He is a person who gives orders, not a person who asks for help. Given the traditional lower-class status of eunuchs in society at this time, his place in the world is probably hard-fought and embattled. It must be excruciatingly difficult to admit that this is a question he can't answer for himself. And yet, the Ethiopian asks. And God has placed Philip in the exact right place at the exact right time to preach the Good News yet again.

The Ethiopian's request for guidance seems right out of the catechism from *The Book of Common Prayer*, which tells us, "We understand the meaning of the Bible by the help of the Holy Spirit, who guides the Church in the true interpretation of the Scriptures." This is a fundamental Episcopal philosophy. We don't rely on our individual interpretations of our scripture reading, and we don't rely on a church leader to tell us what we believe. We rely on the Holy Spirit, who guides the church as one body to the correct understanding, to faithful discernment within community. The Ethiopian joins Philip to wrestle with the text from Isaiah, and they both come to a fuller understanding of the word of God.

The Ethiopian, reading that "out of his anguish he shall see light" (Isaiah 53:11), finds his own heart burning to know the bearer of this hope. The Holy Spirit twice nudges Philip to make sure he meets this man. But here we find a more intimate moment, human to human; Philip connects scripture and the longing of the eunuch's heart to proclaim to him wholeness by joining himself to the living and the dead in the Body of Christ.

The power of the gospel to restore dignity to a man judged unworthy makes the suddenness of the Ethiopian's next request of Philip less surprising than it might be. Seeing water, he asks to be baptized, and Philip agrees. As the Ethiopian emerges from the water (we aren't told if it's a stream or a lake, or even a puddle), Philip disappears, snatched away by the Holy Spirit. Because of his willingness to forgo his own comfort, to go into places where he might not be welcome in order to preach the good news, Philip is sent forth to spread the gospel to every town he encounters along his journey. As bewildering as this must be, the Ethiopian remains a person reborn, and he goes "on his way, rejoicing."

CHAPTER 7: SCRIPTURE
STEVE PANKEY

The story of Philip and the Ethiopian eunuch is compelling for many reasons. Of course, the main character is a bit unusual, being both a foreigner and a eunuch. In biblical times, eunuchs were men who had been castrated and were often slaves or servants. However, the Ethiopian eunuch has social standing as the treasurer for the queen. Another noteworthy detail is his possession of a book. Books were rare in the first century. So was the ability to read, for that matter. Owning a copy of a manuscript was the exclusive privilege of the elite.

So, this story is about an Ethiopian eunuch reading from a scroll containing the words of the Prophet Isaiah. I don't know the odds, but I'd bet Philip has a better chance of winning the lottery than happening upon this scene. And yet here is the Ethiopian eunuch asking Philip a singular question, one I hear echoed in my ministry: How should I read the Bible? Or as the Ethiopian eunuch phrases the question, "How am I to understand unless someone guides me?"

Let me begin answering this question by saying unequivocally that reading the Bible is a spiritual discipline to which every Christian is called. As baptized members of the Body of Christ, our primary identity is that of Jesus' disciples, which comes from the Latin word for student. As students of the Way, we are called to engage in the stories of God's salvation by turning to the Bible for our own spiritual growth.

The Bible is a rich tapestry of poetry, myth, history, song, narrative, and theology that tells the story of God's loving plan for humanity. While some parts may seem frighteningly intense or dreadfully boring, it is, in the end, an intimate love story between the God of All Creation and the humanity God creates in God's own image. Reading the Bible on a regular basis opens up the fullness of this love story and helps us to grow in our knowledge of God.

For some of us, the Bible might awaken our curiosity and call us to find guides to help us understand what God is saying to us, just as the Ethiopian is found by Philip. For others, a sudden revelation might lead us to make a deeper commitment to our faith, like baptism or a new ministry. For others, reading the Bible helps us remember God's love for us, imparting comfort and strength for our daily lives or simply filling us with joy and a longing to know Christ more deeply.

Just because we read the Bible doesn't mean we always understand it. The reality of the Bible's difficult passages makes the eunuch's question all the more valid—and important. How can we understand unless someone guides us? Without a biblical scholar on standby, it can feel intimidating to open the Bible. *The Book of Common Prayer* offers a wonderful approach to biblical engagement in the form of a prayer:

Blessed Lord, who caused all holy Scriptures to be written for our learning: Grant us so to hear them, read, mark, learn, and inwardly digest them, that we may embrace and ever hold fast the blessed hope of everlasting life, which you have given us in our Savior Jesus Christ; who lives and reigns with you and the Holy Spirit, one God, for ever and ever. *Amen.*

From this prayer, we glean six principles for reading the Bible:

1. It was written for our learning
2. It is best heard
3. It is also to be read
4. We should dig deep
5. Digestion takes time
6. Its end is the blessed hope of everlasting life

Let's unpack each of these principles.

WRITTEN FOR OUR LEARNING

One of the Bible's primary purposes is educational. We learn from the Bible that God creates us, God loves us, God wants what is best for us, and God goes ridiculously out of the way to be in relationship with us. In return, there are expectations of how we should live by sharing the love of God in word and deed with our neighbors.

Some people claim to be biblical literalists—that every word of scripture is true and accurate. Others say the Bible is a collection of stories meant solely to inspire.

These two viewpoints set up a false dichotomy. There is deep and profound truth in the Bible, much of it relayed through stories meant to educate and inform. I invite you not to get stuck on whether every detail of John's Revelation should be read literally and instead immerse yourself in the deep truth of scripture, letting the Word of God teach and guide you.

BEST HEARD

When I was in seminary, we discussed the theory of primacy of place. That is, those things listed first in a series of options should be considered the most desirable. If we follow that thought, then the prayer—*Grant us to hear them*—hints that the best way to engage scriptures is through listening to them. For centuries, these biblical stories were passed orally from one generation to the next. The story of God was woven in with the story of God's people. Parents told children who told their children. These were the stories shared around the well or fire—the proverbial water cooler—stories that saturated every aspect of life. With the rise of the printed word and increased levels of literacy, these living, breathing stories became canonized. The stories could be recalled without constant repetition. They sat on shelves next to other texts, waiting to be read aloud. When we hear the word of God, we inhabit the experience of our ancestors. We hear the story of God's love in new ways. We experience it through the voice of our neighbor. In hearing the Word read, we are reminded of our place in the community of God.

AND ALSO READ

Christians are also called to read the Bible for their own spiritual growth. We should read the Bible every day. How we approach reading the Bible is up to each individual. Some people read the whole Bible cover to cover, starting with Genesis and ending with Revelation. Several reading plans exist for reading the entire Bible in ninety days, one year, or longer. Some plans jump back and forth between the Old and New Testaments, while others try to follow a chronological order. It might take some time to find the model that is right for you but keep at it.

Others may wish to engage the scriptures by following the Episcopal lectionary, a prescribed list of readings that includes a significant portion of the Old and New Testaments read over a two-year period. The Daily Office, which consists of two main daily prayer services, morning and evening prayer, offers the opportunity to read all 150 psalms every seven weeks as well as significant portions of the Old Testament and New Testament over the course of two years. The Daily Office lectionary is useful for both beginners and biblical experts, joining the reader with thousands of Episcopalians around the world who read the same lessons every day.[3]

---

[3] The Daily Office Lectionary can be found in *The Book of Common Prayer*, beginning on page 936.

DIG DEEP

The fourth principle of our prayer teaches us is to mark or go deeper in our study of scripture. The word mark isn't used this way much anymore, but in the prayer, it means to make note of or pay special attention to something. As you read the Bible, words or phrases may jump out at you. Even after fifteen years of studying the Bible with regularity, I hear and read things that seem to hit me for the first time. Just last night, at our campus ministry evening prayer service, I noticed that nobody has eaten for three days when Jesus feeds the 4,000 in the Gospel of Matthew. This detail opened up all sorts of imagery for me, alluding to Jonah's three days in the belly of the fish and Jesus' three days in the tomb. I have likely heard this lesson read aloud or read it myself a dozen times in the last decade, and yet, it became brand new to me. This is what the author of Hebrews means by saying, "The word of God is living and active."

Every time we read a passage from scripture, we do so with a new set of lenses. Our life experiences have changed, even if it is just a day later, and we see the text afresh. Because scripture is living and active, the Bible shows itself to us in different ways, opening up new meanings and helping us to grow our knowledge of God and our relationship with God. As we read these sacred texts, we ought to mark those things that give us pause as places where God may be trying to teach us something new, expand our understanding, and invite us into deeper faith.

INWARDLY DIGEST

Coming to a deep understanding rarely happens immediately. Instead, as we mark these things that catch us anew, we are invited and encouraged to chew on them for a while. For Ezekiel and Jeremiah, two prophets of the Old Testament, God commands them to literally eat the scrolls. The same is true for John of Patmos in his vision of the Revelation. Eating something assumes that it will be inwardly digested, and digestion takes time.

I am not a physician, but I know there are lots of twists and turns in the digestive tract. The process of retrieving nutrients from food is not a fast one but rather takes place through the deliberate work of muscles, enzymes, and companion organs. The same is true with gaining meaning and nourishment from the Bible. It takes time and can require some outside help. These sources could include a Bible commentary, reputable website, study group, or clergy person. Remember: the primary way we are to engage scripture is in community, so be ready to check your interpretation with that of someone you trust.

BLESSED HOPE

Finally, we ask ourselves, to what end do we read the Bible? What is the ultimate goal of reading scripture, of hearing, reading, marking, learning, and inwardly digesting the Word of God? The prayer offers this answer: "That we may embrace and ever hold fast the blessed hope of everlasting life." A phrase included in every consecration and ordination service for bishops, priests, and deacons since the English Reformation explains that the Holy Scriptures of the Old and New Testament "contain all things necessary to salvation."

Within the pages of the Bible, we learn everything we need to know about God's saving grace for humanity. We learn we were made in the image of God, sin has created a breach in what was designed to be a perfect relationship, and God continually seeks to bring us back into right relationship. We learn that by the grace of God, through the saving work accomplished in the life, death, and resurrection of Jesus, we have access to the God of love. We learn that in the end, God's desire is wholeness, peace, *shalom*. The journey there is difficult and fraught with stories of humanity's failures. It is bloody, sad, and will make you doubt your faith at moments.

You may find yourself like the Ethiopian eunuch, in need of someone to guide you. Accept the help of the Philips in your life. Make time to hear the Bible read aloud in community. Read it on your own, take time to let it sink in, and check your understanding with those you trust. And no matter what, read scripture, believing that above all else, God's saving love is revealed within its pages.

FOR REFLECTION AND DISCUSSION

- What new insights into hearing and reading the Bible struck you in this chapter?

- What is your favorite Bible passage? What does it mean to you?

- What might be different in your congregation if everyone read the Bible daily and talked with at least one other person about what they read each week?

- How have you experienced the love of God through engagement with the scripture?

FOR ACTION

- Next Sunday during worship, put your leaflet down, close your eyes, and listen to the words of scripture being read. Then reflect: What did you hear that was new? What did you feel was missing? Imagine what it would be like if we didn't have Bibles in every house. How would this change your experience of God?

- Begin to read, mark, learn, and inwardly digest the scriptures by finding a Bible study partner. For a three-month period, commit to reading the same passages of scripture each day and check in with one another at the end of each week.

CHAPTER 8: KNOWING THE COMMUNITY
FRANK LOGUE

Encompassed by the Vaca Mountains on the east and the Mayacamas rising more than 2,000 feet to the west, California's Napa Valley enjoys a long growing season with days of warm sun followed by cool evenings. Within this viticultural kingdom are fourteen microclimates where the crops benefit from uniquely hotter, drier air in one area and cooler, foggier mornings in another. Beyond this, the land is quite diverse as the changes in sea level, volcanic eruptions, and the grinding of tectonic plates over the last sixty million years formed at least thirty different types of soil.

The task of the winemaker is to become intimately familiar with the soil in the vineyard and the particular microclimate, planting almost black Cabernet Sauvignon grapes in one sunny area and placing delicate pink Gewürztraminer grapes in a cooler zone. The harvest depends on discovering and then attending to the particularity of each place.

Each congregation works within a unique corner of the vast vineyard that is the kingdom of God. Though the good news of Jesus is the same in all the contexts in which we find ourselves, how a congregation embodies the gospel can and will vary.

Throughout the Acts of the Apostles, we follow the ways in which the nascent faith in Jesus is formed in new contexts. In the eighth chapter of Acts, the church experiences centrifugal force as the Holy Spirit sends the disciples outward. At the end of that chapter, an angel of the Lord dispatches Philip to a wilderness road between Jerusalem and Gaza. Philip comes to join an Ethiopian eunuch returning home from worshiping in Jerusalem. The man is reading one of the "suffering servant" passages in the Prophet Isaiah, "Like a sheep he was led to the slaughter, and like a lamb silent before its shearer, so he does not open his mouth." Starting with that passage, Philip explains the good news of Jesus to this stranger.

The man reading from Isaiah in his chariot comes from what those in the Roman Empire considered "the ends of the earth." And as the eunuch and Philip come to water, the Ethiopian asks, "What is to prevent me from being baptized?" The simple answer could have been, "Being a eunuch prevents your baptism." According to Deuteronomy 23:1, people with genital mutilation were not able to fully take part in temple worship.

The Ethiopian eunuch is quite a test case for a follower of Jesus. As a Jewish rabbi, Jesus behaves scandalously in touching people who cannot participate in temple worship, including a leper (Luke 5:12-14) and a woman who has been suffering from hemorrhages for twelve years (Luke 8:43-48). Like these other outcasts, a more judgmental follower could see the Ethiopian as too "other" for baptism. Even as the Holy Spirit snatches

Philip away to Azotus, the good news of Jesus begins stretching beyond Judea as this new convert heads south on the wilderness road home.

From this point onward, the followers of Jesus who have been sent out as apostles continually come across new settings. By the time Paul is preaching in Athens (Acts 17), we see him beginning with the faith he finds already present in those to whom he preaches:

"Athenians, I see how extremely religious you are in every way. For as I went through the city and looked carefully at the objects of your worship, I found among them an altar with the inscription, 'To an unknown god.' What therefore you worship as unknown, this I proclaim to you."

In the same way, congregations today need to start with people where they are. As Jesus meets the needs of the people, so too do churches need to start with the needs of those around them. And as the apostles customize their way of proclaiming the gospel to the audiences that gathered, we also need to find ways to embody the timeless message of God in Christ for the people we meet.

A demographic study is one important way to find eyes to see the community around you. An Internet search can lead to good demographics on your area available through the United States Census Bureau, but there are companies that can dig deeper into the data through additional research. Percept and MissionInsite are two companies that specialize in providing demographic data targeted to churches.[4] I have used reports from both companies, and they have been extremely useful in getting to know a community. Their reports are worth the relatively small costs.

To compare how different the contexts can be, take the example of two coastal Georgia congregations—Christ Church Frederica on Saint Simons Island and King of Peace in Kingsland. The churches are exactly forty-five miles apart, yet they represent very different realities.

The population around Christ Church is almost entirely white. Half of the population makes more than $100,000 per year, with an average household income of $107,392. Fifty-eight percent of the people have a bachelor's degree or higher.

In Kingsland, 68 percent of the community is white, with significant numbers of African Americans and Latinos. The household income average is $66,713, with 30 percent of households under $50,000 per year. Just 30 percent of the people have a bachelor's degree or higher.

This quick snapshot shows the differences between the two communities, with Saint Simons Island inhabited by many white-collar retirees and Kingsland largely populated by blue-collar working families. The gospel is

---

[4] Episcopal congregations can find summary demographic reports from MissionInsite for the 3-mile radius surrounding their church on the Episcopal Church website by inputting their diocese and congregation here: https://pr.dfms.org/studyyourcongregation/.

the same in each location, but there can be differences in how a church embodies that good news for its community.

I learned this as a seminarian at St. Philip's in Baden, Maryland. The historically black church had an average Sunday attendance of forty-four when I arrived. I had asked the person in charge of field education to introduce me to the smallest church that was vital to its community. This rural church hosted the clothes closet and food pantry for the community. They had received a grant for a transportation ministry to pick people up at their homes and take them to the doctor, grocery store, or other essential trips. This small congregation had also created an eight-bed assisted living facility, so the elderly could stay close to their homes and families when they could no longer care for themselves. The church might have been small in membership and practically flat in growth, adding a single new parishioner in my year with the congregation. But if the doors of the church closed, the community would have had a sizeable hole to fill. St. Philip's would have been deeply missed.

By the time I graduated from seminary to go start a new church, I knew I wanted that church to be a particular kind of place. I wanted to do something so big for God that if God was not in it, we would fall flat on our faces and look like idiots. Because if that was true, then God would have done something in our midst and no one could ever say we had built a church under our own steam. Thinking of St. Philip's, Baden, and its ministries, I also wanted to start a congregation so vital to its community that if the church closed its doors in ten years, people who had never attended the church would miss it and wish it were still open.

The then-Bishop of Georgia, Henry Louttit, had the idea of a new Episcopal church in Kingsland, Georgia, which could reach young families who made up the bulk of the community thanks to Kings Bay Submarine Base and service sector jobs. The town had 8,500 people in the city limits with 25,000 people living within a ten-mile radius. Two other Episcopal churches were ten and eleven miles away from the proposed new congregation.

As I was preparing to leave seminary to start the new church, I ordered a demographic study of my new community. I looked at that data with experienced church planters who gave me eyes to see the uniqueness of the place. Then I studied the maps from the report, which showed where different demographic groups lived. I mapped out a plan for knocking on 100 doors, selected as demographically representative of the town. When people answered the door, I said, "I'm here to start a new Episcopal church. I don't want you to come to the church; I just want to know what a church can do for this community."

After knocking on doors, I asked to be added to the meeting agenda for the Kingsland City Council. I told them about my experience in knocking on doors, shared what I learned, and asked them the same question. Not only did speaking to the city council garner good press for our new church, but council members asked me to start their meetings with prayer. For years, I attended council meetings, opening the gatherings in prayer. This practice put me in regular contact with the mayor and council as well as the chief of police, fire chief, and other city officials and leaders. Those relationships led to my being more of a pastor to the community than would have been open to me without that routine contact.

So, what did I learn about the community in the process? Lots of people told me the area needed more activities for children and teens and that it needed a sense of community. I learned about the pressing need for a full-day preschool for families with two working parents. I also saw that the small group I was gathering had the skills needed to undertake the project.

These conversations led to the creation of a full day preschool. Meeting this need transformed the heart of the church. New people arrived, bringing their gifts and experiences. In time we added thriving scouting programs as God gave us the people with the right gifts and passion. A two-night-a-week Narcotics Anonymous meeting founded by church members followed.

After coming to know the community through a combination of demographic data and conversations started by knocking on doors, I dove deeper. I talked to submariners about working months at a time largely underwater. I was able to tour a submarine, and I spent time learning about leadership from the base commander whose wife served with me on the Habitat for Humanity board. I learned about the ebbs and flows of families dealing with the continuous deployment of a ballistic missile sub, where crews spent three to four months at sea and three to four months in port.

A nearby paper mill employed nearly 1,000 people. I tried to learn about life in the mill from families who knew it well. Poor maintenance led to increasing problems, culminating in an explosion that killed one person and left two severely damaged for life. The mill closed, and I joined with other pastors to hold a series of worship services in the mill marking the occasion for each of the final shifts. We then worked together to provide support for families needing to move away or find very different vocations. The community I served was very different from the retirees living just up the coast.

I once called a new seminary graduate to work with me in Kingsland. He had been a youth minister at a large church in Atlanta. He arrived talking about how well he understood the challenges teens faced with their over-programmed lives and their efforts to stand out as applicants to top colleges. He arrived to find the lives of the teens in Kingsland very different. The high school dropout rate and teen pregnancy were more of an issue, and I never met any teen looking to get into an Ivy League school. The teens he knew in Atlanta and the teens he met in Camden County, Georgia, all needed Jesus, but the particular way they experienced that grace was not the same.

Just as no Napa Valley winegrower would plant the same grapes in different areas, the way we go about the work of the gospel depends on the location in which we serve. As you read this book, you are placed in a specific environment. The gospel is not found in the general but the particular, where the universal truth of Jesus is experienced.

PROVEN METHODS OF CONNECTING

Here are some other ideas for getting to know your community:

- Schedule one-on-one meetings with community leaders, including school principals, leaders of social service agencies, church leaders from other denominations, government officials, and the Chamber of Commerce and other business leaders. Ask these folks about their life stories and values. Spend time listening to them and ask what key issues they see in the community and how a church might help

- Take a prayerwalk to see the community through gospel eyes even as you pray for the people and their needs

- Volunteer as a chaplain for the police, fire department, or community hospital

- Offer bottles of water at community events as a way of serving your neighbors

- Work with other groups on public events like a Blessing of the Animals at the Humane Society or a Blessing of the Backpacks at a breakfast before the first day of school

- Respond to local, national, or world tragedies by gathering an ecumenical group for prayer

- Work with others in the community to create community leader breakfasts or lunches with speakers and follow-up conversations about neighborhood issues

FOR REFLECTION AND DISCUSSION

- What new ideas struck you in this chapter?

- When have you experienced God moving you to do something or to speak to someone similar to the way the Holy Spirit prompts Philip to speak to the Ethiopian?

- How does your congregation discover who is in the surrounding community and what their needs are?

- What group of people in your community has very different life experiences from you? How might you come to understand what their lives are like? What might their experience be if they showed up at your church Sunday morning?

- In what ways is the microclimate where your church ministers different from a congregation an hour away? How might this change how you embody the gospel?

FOR ACTION

Print a demographic study of your community and take the following steps:

- Note how your congregation reflects or differs from the median population of your area in terms of ethnicity, income, education, and other statistics.

- Notice how those in leadership in your church reflect the surrounding community.

- Think about how the ministries of the congregation reflect the needs of the community highlighted in the demographics.

- Set up an interview with a couple of leaders in your community and ask about their life stories, the needs they see in the community, and how your church might help. Share what you learn with others in your congregation.

- Take a neighborhood prayerwalk with a small group of people. If possible, walk. If not, drive to key places where you can look anew, listen closely, and offer prayer. The goal is to notice who is around and what God is already doing. Imagine how your congregation might join with the Holy Spirit as you work with your neighbors on community needs.

CONCLUSION:
EVANGELISM IN RELATIONSHIP
CARRIE BOREN HEADINGTON

The Book of Acts commences with the final words spoken by the resurrected Jesus to his followers before he ascends into Heaven, "The Holy Spirit will come upon you and you will be my witnesses in Jerusalem, in all Judea, in Samaria, and to the ends of the earth." The Book of Acts is the story of God, the great evangelist, and God's people, the church, living out God's call. This evangelistic commission from the Book of Acts is the same call to God's people today.

Jesus fully reveals God to us and then says to his followers, "Now you will be my witnesses." Essentially Jesus was saying, *Now you will be my hands, my feet, my compassion, my healing, my justice, my love, my power, my peace, my mouthpiece, my life on this earth until I come again.* This book has explored how we can learn from the first followers of Jesus who shared the good news of God in Jesus Christ in the midst of great challenges and obstacles. The topics covered in this book—reading the signs of the times, worship, proclamation of the message, loving and serving the community, repentance, prayer, reading scripture, and getting to know the community—all serve the primary mission of the church and the call of all followers of Jesus to share the good news with the whole creation through word and deed.

As our *Book of Common Prayer* states, "The mission of the Church is to restore all people to unity with God and each other in Christ...The Church pursues its mission as it prays and worships, proclaims the Gospel, and promotes justice, peace, and love...The church carries out its mission through the ministry of all its members."

Our Baptismal Covenant asks, "Will you proclaim in word and example the good news of God in Christ?" We respond: "We will, with God's help."

We are called to know Christ and to make him known. This is evangelism. This is the mission of the church. The church is the community, the Body of Christ, called to share the good news of Jesus with the world.

Many Episcopalians balk at the word evangelism. I know I have in the past. We sometimes cringe at the word because our perception of evangelism is that it's intrusive, pushy, impolite, and sometimes downright rude. But when Jesus asks his followers to witness for him in the Book of Acts, he has something else in mind. Jesus wants us to spread good news—that God is real, that God is alive, that God wants to be in a life-transforming eternal relationship with all people, and that this relationship has been made possible through the reconciling action of Jesus Christ.

The principles from the Book of Acts on how to engage in evangelism are as relevant today as they were 2,000 years ago. Within thirty years after Jesus' resurrection, the good news of Christ spread throughout the world. And this was without social media, plane travel, and the Internet! I believe these evangelists were infused with four key factors, traits that can guide and support us as we spread the good news in our own day and age.

MOTIVATION

The first followers of Jesus are so enlivened by their encounter with the resurrected Jesus they cannot be silenced. The good news bubbles out of them. When Peter and John are told to stay silent, they reply, "We cannot keep from speaking about what we have seen and heard" (Acts 4:20).

The followers of Jesus gossip about the gospel. The good news of Jesus spreads through much of the known world with one person telling another person who tells another. The news of Jesus spreads like wildfire! Evangelism is not a program but a natural part of everyday life as people engage in relationships with others. Sharing Jesus is as natural as sharing the location of a good water well. While Acts contains a few examples of people speaking to large groups, the message spreads primarily by followers of Jesus talking with friends and family about their experience of the risen Lord and inviting others to meet him as well.

Evangelist and scholar Michael Green said, "Evangelism is overflow." The church needs motivation more than new methods. The followers in Acts do not need evangelism courses. Why? Their faith is so emboldened by the gospel that it spills out of them wherever they go in daily life.

One can palpably sense their enthusiasm in their words, "We declare to you what was from the beginning, what we have heard, what we have seen with our eyes, what we have looked at and touched with our hands, concerning the word of life—this life was revealed, and we have seen it and testify to it...We are writing these things so that our joy may be complete" (1 John 1:1-4).

Evangelism is a joyous endeavor even in the midst of severe persecution. We discussed in Chapter 1 the challenge of spiritual apathy. The church needs to be honest about this dangerous attitude, and the call to church leaders is to help Episcopalians see God at work in their lives—and to tell others about this divine presence.

MISSION

Early followers of the Way clearly understand their call to evangelize. They are a people commissioned to share the good news of Jesus everywhere they go with whomever they meet.

Today's Episcopal Church, however, has two primary challenges in the area of mission. First, the demands in our individual lives and the life of the congregation cause us to make less time available for others. Second, evangelism has become professionalized and clericalized. Evangelism is no longer embraced as a ministry for the entire Body of Christ as it is in the book of Acts. Many lay Episcopalians genuinely do not know they are commissioned missionaries wherever in the world God has placed them.

When I was a child growing up in the Episcopal church, I remember hoping my priest knew I had new neighbors so he could invite them to church. I did not see reaching out to my neighbors, talking about the gospel, or inviting anyone to church as my job. That was the priest's job!

More than 85 percent of people come to their faith through personal contact with a Christian friend or family member. New signage, exciting parish programs, or even a dynamic priest can help people strengthen and deepen their faith, but the first and critical invitation comes from everyday followers of Jesus forming relationships with people—praying, loving, and sharing Jesus.

We need to reorder and reorient our lives and the life of the congregation. Our worship should culminate in the sending. We are fed with the Word and the Body and Blood of Jesus, so we can then feed others out in the world. We are sent, as our worship ends, to, "Go in peace to love and serve the Lord." We are a people with a mission to share good news. As Archbishop of Canterbury William Temple said, "The church is the only society that exists for the benefit of those who are not its members."

METHOD

All missions in Acts begin with prayer. The people of the Way follow the example of Jesus who teaches, "the harvest is plentiful but the laborers are few, therefore ask the Lord of the harvest to send out laborers into his harvest" (Matthew 9:37-38). Jesus moves to a quiet place to draw near to his heavenly Father and to draw strength from the Holy Spirit. The followers in Acts draw near to the Lord, praying for discernment, wisdom, direction, boldness, and strength. As we draw near to God in prayer, we are led by the Spirit who shows us who to love and how best to love them. A good evangelism model for today is prayer, care, share. Pray for people God has placed around us in daily life. Ask God how to best care for and serve them, and then pray to God to give us the words to share the good news with them.

The early Christians heed the words of Jesus to go to Jerusalem, Judea, Samaria, and to the ends of the earth. This strategy challenges them to intentionally evangelize friends and family and then to stretch beyond, ministering to people, even strangers or those they viewed as enemies. The followers of the Way are flexible and rely on the Holy Spirit to show them how best to share the spiritual journey with others. They go to the ends of the earth, but they begin at home. Our first mission trip is often crossing the street to meet our neighbors.

The third aspect of the early church's method is that they share the good news in both word and action. They share verbally about Jesus, and they engage in actions that today we might call social justice and pastoral care. They heal many people and cast out demons. They feed the hungry and open their homes to strangers from all walks of life. The followers of Jesus are known for their profound love and radical welcome. They show, and they tell. They turn away from the idols of the world (money, success, appearance, and power) and live lives of love and service to others. The quality of their community and their love draws people to them. We need to first love people through our actions to gain the trust to be heard. People will not care what we have to say until they know we care.

MESSAGE

The followers of the Way in the Book of Acts have a message to proclaim. Their message is unequivocal: Jesus Christ was and is the Son of God. He died on the cross for our sins and rose again, reconciling the world to himself. They affirm that Jesus is alive, and the Holy Spirit can be encountered. They speak this message boldly, and they embody this message. They are malleable in the words they use to share the message, but the truth never wavers. The disciples are rooted in the story of the life, death, and resurrection of Jesus and how this witness impacts their own life. They give testimony of their changed lives and tell how their story fuses with God's story. We should never underestimate the power of the gospel message and our own personal faith story.

OUR ACTS TODAY

The Episcopal Church is experiencing a renewed focus on evangelism: the spiritual practice of seeking, naming, and celebrating Jesus' loving presence in everyone's stories, then inviting people to form or deepen their relationship with God in Christ.

More than 2,000 years since the Book of Acts was written, more than 1.7 billion people follow Jesus. From a small band of everyday people facing enormous obstacles, a movement began, and the Lord added to their number day by day. God is the great evangelist. God is the one who draws all people into relationship, and yet, God allows us to be part of this reconciling work. The Book of Acts is filled with people motivated by the Holy Spirit, on a clear mission to share the message of the loving, liberating, life-giving Jesus.

When I received the generous invitation to contribute an afterword to this thoughtful, compelling study of Acts 8, I should have known that I would finally address myself to the task on the Feast of the Annunciation—which was, of course, the deadline given to me. I'm grateful for the push, because it's the right day for the job. In many ways, it is the *Magnificat*—the hymn of Jesus' mother, Mary—that got this whole party started.

Just as the early church described in Acts bears a striking resemblance to our church today, certain aspects of first-century Palestine, too, seem uncomfortably familiar. A vast empire strives for military and economic dominance in distant lands, while its rulers drain resources, co-opt religious leaders, and seek scapegoats to consolidate their base and justify the vast inequality that is the byproduct of their imperialistic control.

Into this world of injustice and violence comes a child whose mother understands before she is even over morning sickness that her son is going to turn the world upside down. "He has shown strength with his arm, he has scattered the proud in their thoughts of their hearts," she sings in Luke 1:51-53. "He has brought down the powerful from their thrones, and lifted up the lowly; he has filled the hungry with good things, and sent the rich away empty."

Fast forward three decades or so. Jesus, just as his mother prophesied, has shaken the empire to its core and been executed by the Roman Empire as a revolutionary. When Acts begins, the empire is trying to finish the job by making sure that the followers of Jesus will not survive to preach another day. But again and again, the Holy Spirit intervenes and sets them and their gospel free.

It is that work of the Holy Spirit that the authors of this book have brought to life, giving us all a faithful, hopeful reading of Acts to guide the church today. Using their interpretations, reflections, and study questions, we can find new, creative ways to unleash the Holy Spirit in our congregations and communities and allow her power to renew our spirits and our passion for sharing the gospel.

You may have surmised, as you read this book, that its authors have done no small thing by inviting the church into Acts. "On the whole, I do not find Christians, outside of the catacombs, sufficiently sensible of conditions...." writes author Annie Dillard in her book, *Teaching a Stone to Talk*. "It is madness to wear ladies' straw hats and velvet hats to church; we should all be wearing crash helmets. Ushers should issue life preservers and signal flares; they should lash us to our pews." It's Acts that most makes me think of Dillard's dictum; she knows that once the Holy Spirit is unleashed, everything is up for grabs. Like the apostles, once we're under the influence of Acts, we might find ourselves doing things we never expected and spending time with people we never encountered before. If we really follow through on what's been suggested to us, we're going to need those crash helmets.

The eminent black liberation theologian James Cone described the stakes. "The Christian gospel is God's message of liberation in an unredeemed and tortured world," he wrote in *The Cross and the Lynching Tree*. But it is also, he said, "an immanent reality—a powerful liberating presence among the poor right *now* in their midst..." Once we enter into Acts—into Stephen's martyrdom at the hands of the empire, into Saul's violent persecutions, into Philip's roadside baptism of someone he just didn't see coming—we open ourselves and the people around us up to liberation. *Right now.* That might just mean the foundations of the church that we know are shaken until the doors fly open. It might mean that those of us inside, like the apostles, are liberated for the work God has given us to do in the midst of today's empire and its wreckage of injustice and cruelty.

When the angel Gabriel appears to Mary, she says, "Here am I, the servant of the Lord; let it be with me according to your word." She might as well have said, *Buckle up and put on your helmet. The Spirit is here, and there's no telling what's going to happen next.*

The Feast of the Annunciation 2018

ABOUT THE EDITORS

Susan Brown Snook serves as canon to the ordinary for church growth and development in the Episcopal Diocese of Oklahoma, leading ministries of congregational development, evangelism, church planting, and spiritual and numerical growth. She also leads a staff team that includes communications, Christian formation, and stewardship. Previously, she was church planter, vicar, and then rector of the Episcopal Church of the Nativity in Scottsdale, Arizona, from 2006 to 2017. Susan received her master of divinity degree from Church Divinity School of the Pacific in 2003 and is currently working toward a doctor of ministry degree from Virginia Theological Seminary. She is a founder and leader of the Acts 8 Movement. She and her husband, Tom, have two amazing daughters.

Adam Trambley is the rector of St. John's Episcopal Church in Sharon, Pennsylvania. He has served as vice president of Sharon City Council and been on the board of the local library, food bank, and Chamber of Commerce. His doctor of ministry thesis project involved taking community leaders on prayerwalks to see where God is at work in their city. He is part of the Acts 8 Movement Steering Committee, a deputy to General Convention, and secretary of the Diocese of Northwestern Pennsylvania. When not working on community redevelopment or church revitalization, Adam is probably in a ballet studio. He and his wife, Jane, have two daughters.

ABOUT THE CONTRIBUTORS

Joseph Alsay serves as rector of St. Augustine of Canterbury Episcopal Church in Oklahoma City. Ordained in the Evangelical Lutheran Church in America, Joseph was received as a priest into the Episcopal Church in 2011. During his ministry at St. Augustine, the congregation has seen its membership triple, finances grow, and racial and ethnic diversity increase. He currently serves as a board member of the Oklahoma Conference of Churches, the Oklahoma Alliance of Liturgy and the Arts, the Society of Catholic Priests, and is the director of the aspirancy program for the Episcopal Diocese of Oklahoma. He and his wife, Cecilia, have three children together and live in Edmond, Oklahoma.

Carrie Boren Headington is an evangelist with a passion to see people come to know the abounding unconditional love of God. She speaks throughout the United States and around the globe, sharing the abundant life found in Jesus Christ with spiritual seekers and Christians alike. Carrie is the founder of The Good News Initiative, which provides resources in evangelism. She works with all Christian denominations and serves as canon for evangelism in the Episcopal Diocese of Dallas and consulting evangelist for Revivals for The Episcopal Church, engaging in evangelistic speaking and apologetics, and equipping congregations to be the hands, feet, and mouthpieces for God in their communities. Carrie is a graduate of Yale University and Harvard University, and has two graduate degrees in theology, evangelism, and apologetics from Oxford University. Carrie is also an adjunct professor of evangelism at Fuller Seminary, an author on evangelism, and frequent blogger.

Frank Logue is an Episcopal priest who assists the bishop in overseeing the seventy congregations of the Diocese of Georgia. He previously worked with his wife, Victoria, daughter, Griffin, and many others to start King of Peace Episcopal Church and Day School in Kingsland, Georgia. He is a member of the Executive Council of the Episcopal Church and also serves on the denomination's advisory group on church planting. Frank enjoys photography, hiking, and travel, often all at the same time.

Brendan O'Sullivan-Hale is canon to the ordinary for administration and evangelism in the Episcopal Diocese of Indianapolis, where he manages finances and operations and supports lay and clergy leaders in developing creative strategies to observe how God is acting in the communities where they serve and responding faithfully with the good news of Jesus

Christ. He was previously a partner at a midwestern wealth management firm. He is a member of the Episcopal Church of All Saints, Indianapolis. Together with Holli Powell, he co-hosted "The Collect Call," a podcast about *The Book of Common Prayer.*

Steve Pankey is the rector of Christ Episcopal Church in Bowling Green, Kentucky. He has served the wider Episcopal Church as a two-time deputy to General Convention and a member of the Task Force on Leveraging Social Media for Evangelism. Steve holds a master of divinity degree from Virginia Theological Seminary and a doctor of ministry degree from the School of Theology at the University of the South. As a disciple, a husband to Cassie, a father to Eliza and Lainey, and a rector, Steve struggles to keep it all in the right order and is constantly thankful for forgiveness and grace. You can read more from him at his blog, draughtingtheology. wordpress.com.

Holli Powell is an amateur photographer, a lay preacher and theologian, a Microsoft Excel wizard, and a member of the Episcopal Church's Executive Council. She has devoted her career to nonprofit finances, currently serving as the vice president of finance and operations for MACED, an organization working with people in Appalachia to create economic opportunity. She lives with her partner, their two children, and their two cats in Lexington, Kentucky.

ABOUT FORWARD MOVEMENT

Forward Movement is committed to inspiring disciples and empowering evangelists. Our ministry is lived out by creating resources such as books, small-group studies, apps, and conferences. Our daily devotional, *Forward Day by Day*, is also available in Spanish (*Adelante Dia a Dia*) and Braille, online, as a podcast, and as an app for smartphones or tablets. It is mailed to more than fifty countries, and we donate nearly 30,000 copies each quarter to prisons, hospitals, and nursing homes.

We actively seek partners across the church and look for ways to provide resources that inspire and challenge. A ministry of the Episcopal Church for over eighty years, Forward Movement is a nonprofit organization funded by sales of resources and by gifts from generous donors.

To learn more about Forward Movement and our resources, visit www.ForwardMovement.org. We are delighted to be doing this work and invite your prayers and support.